Presented to

Martha Peterson

On the occasion of

National Day of Prayer

From

Pines Bible Church
4274 W Dunes Hwy
Michigan City IN 46360
219-874-6997
Date

May 6   2004

Contributing editors: Daniel P. Anderson, Douglas Ed Cox, and Edward A. Elliott Sr. Style editor: Carol Rebell

Published by Humble Creek, P.O. Box 719, Uhrichsville, Ohio 44683

Printed in the United States of America.

5 4 3 2

GOD'S WORD FOR

P Growing in Prayer

Compiled from the works of
Andrew Murray

HUMBLECREEK
INSPIRATION FOR LIFE

GOD'S WORD FOR

Growing in Prayer

From Day to Day

*Though our bodies are dying,
our spirits are being renewed every day.*

2 Corinthians 4:16

All Christians, young or old, must learn the absolute necessity of fellowship with Jesus each day. This lesson is not always taught at the beginning of the Christian life. The grace we have received of the forgiveness of sins and of joy in the Holy Spirit can only be preserved by daily renewal in fellowship with Jesus Christ Himself.

Many Christians backslide because this truth is not clearly taught. Some are unable to stand against temptation or their old nature. Though they strive to do their best to fight against sin and to serve God, they have no strength. They have never really grasped the secret that the Lord Jesus will continue His work in the believer every day from heaven. But there is one condition: Time alone with the Lord Jesus each day is the indispensable condition of growth and power.

Read Matthew 11:25–30. Listen to Christ's word: "Come to Me. . .and I will give you rest. . . . Let me teach you. . .and you will find rest for your souls." Let the Lord teach you just how gentle and humble He is. Bow before Him, tell Him that you need Him and His love; He will let His love rest on you. This applies not only to young Christians but to all who love the Lord.

Dear Lord, I want to please You. Enable me to enjoy this blessed experience of fellowship with You each day. Help me learn the lesson to spend time daily—without exception—in fellowship with You. Amen.

FELLOWSHIP WITH GOD

I have loved you even as the Father has loved me.
Remain in my love.

JOHN 15:9

The three Persons in the Godhead are the Father, the Son, and the Holy Spirit—each one is different from the others. God desires to reveal Himself as a person. Each one of us is an individual distinct from others and standing in certain relationships to others. God will reveal Himself to us as a person, and we are called to enter into fellowship with Him.

God greatly desires this relationship with us, but sin has come between us and our God. Even in Christians who know God, there is often great ignorance and even indifference to this personal relationship of love to God.

People believe that at conversion their sins are forgiven, that God accepts them so that they may go to heaven, and that they should try to do God's will. But they do not realize that, even as a father and his child on earth enjoy being together, so they must have this intimate fellowship with God each day.

Our relationship to Christ rests on His deep, tender love to us. We are not capable on our own to render Him this love, but the Holy Spirit will do the work in us. Meditate quietly on this thought: "And because they love me, my Father will love them, and I will love them" (John 14:21). Take time to experience this personal fellowship.

Lord, You have loved me so much. I earnestly desire to love You above all. Amen.

JESUS

You are to name him Jesus,
for he will save his people from their sins.

MATTHEW 1:21

The Lord Jesus was a person on this earth. He had His own individual name. His mother, His disciples, all His friends called Him by this name—Jesus. But they probably thought little of what that name meant. Nor do the majority of Christians know what a treasure is contained in that name—Jesus—"He shall save His people from their sins."

Many think about His death on the cross and His resurrection, but do they realize that He is a living person in heaven who thinks of us each day? He wants us to bring Him our love and worship.

When we first ask Jesus Christ to save us from our sins, we know very little about how this is done. The living Christ reveals Himself to us, and through the power of His love, our desire to sin is taken away. Through personal fellowship with Him, Jesus saves us from our sins. First we must come to Jesus confessing all the sin in our hearts. We must know Him as the almighty personal Savior in whom God's holiness dwells. As we fellowship together in the expression of mutual love, by the work of His Holy Spirit in our hearts, His love will expel and conquer all the sin.

O Lord, may I learn the joyfulness of each day in fellowship with You, finding the secret of happiness and holiness. May I learn to go apart with You each day and experience Your presence, enabling me to love and serve You and to walk in Your ways. In Jesus' name, amen.

ALONE WITH GOD

When you pray, go away by yourself,
shut the door behind you,
and pray to your Father secretly.

MATTHEW 6:6

Have you ever thought what a wonderful privilege it is to have the liberty of asking God to meet with you and to hear what you have to say? We should use such a privilege gladly and faithfully.

"When you pray," says Jesus, "go away by yourself, shut the door behind you, and pray to your Father secretly." This means two things. (1) Shut the world out; withdraw from all the thoughts and concerns of the day. (2) Shut yourself in alone with God to pray in secret. Let this be your chief object in prayer, to realize the presence of your heavenly Father. Let your goal be: "Alone with God."

Being alone in His presence and praying to the Father in secret is only the beginning. Come to Him in the full assurance that He knows how you long for His help and guidance. He will listen to you.

Then follows the great promise of verse 6: "Then your Father, who knows all secrets, will reward you." Your Father will see to it that your prayer is not in vain. Prayer in secret will be followed by the secret working of God in my heart.

Lord Jesus, thank You for the promise of Your presence, and show me the way to be alone with You. Help me to be childlike and trustful in my fellowship with You, confessing each sin and bringing You my every need. Amen.

THE IMPORTANCE OF FAITH

"Don't be afraid. Just trust me."

MARK 5:36

This is a lesson of the greatest importance. When praying alone in the presence of God, we must trust implicitly in the love of God and in the power of the Lord Jesus. Take time to ask yourself this question: Is my heart full of a steadfast faith in God's love? If this is not the case, focus on this before you begin to pray. Faith does not come of itself.

Consider quietly how impossible it is for God to lie. He is ready with infinite love to give you His blessing. Take some text of Scripture in which God's power, faithfulness, and love are revealed. Apply the words and say: "Yes, Lord, I will pray with firm faith in You."

It is a mistake to limit the word "faith" to the forgiveness of sins and to our acceptance as children of God. Faith includes far more. We must have faith in all that God is willing to do for us. We must have faith according to our special needs. Jesus Christ gives grace for each new day, and our faith must reach out according to the needs of the day.

When you enter into the Father's presence and before you begin to pray, ask yourself: "Do I really believe that God is here with me and that the Lord Jesus will help me to pray?" Jesus often taught His disciples how indispensable faith was to true prayer. He will teach us as well.

Lord Jesus, teach me this lesson. Strengthen my faith in Your almighty power. May I see the glory of God, for I ask in Your name, amen.

Obey the Word of God

People need more than bread for their life;
they must feed on every word of God.

Matthew 4:4

B read is indispensable to life. We all understand this. However strong a person may be, if he takes no nourishment he will grow weaker and eventually die. Even so with the Word of God.

Bread must be eaten. I may know all about bread. I may give it to others. I may have bread in my house and on my table in great abundance, but that will not help me. I must eat the bread. If through illness I am unable to eat it, I shall die. Likewise, mere knowledge of God's Word and even preaching it to others will not help me. It is not enough to think about it. I must feed on God's Word and take it into my heart and life.

Bread must be eaten daily, and the same is true of God's Word. The psalmist says: "They delight in doing everything the LORD wants; day and night they think about his law" (Psalm 1:2). "Oh, how I love your law! I think about it all day long" (Psalm 119:97). To secure a strong and powerful spiritual life, spending time in God's Word every day is indispensable. When on earth the Lord Jesus learned, loved, and obeyed the word of the Father. If you seek fellowship with Him, you will find Him in His Word.

Lord Jesus Christ, please teach me to fellowship with the Father through the Word, even as You did. Teach me to live solely for the glory of God and the fulfillment of His Word. Amen.

THE WORD AND PRAYER

Restore my life again, just as you promised.

PSALM 119:107

Prayer and the Word of God are inseparable and should always go together. In His Word God speaks to me, and in prayer I speak to God. If there is to be true communication, God and I must both take part. If I simply pray without using God's Word, I am apt to use my own words and thoughts. Taking God's thoughts from His Word and presenting them before Him really gives prayer its power. God's Word is indispensable for all true prayer!

Through the Word the Holy Spirit shows me who God is. The Word also teaches me how sinful I am. It reveals to me all the wonders that God will do for me and the strength He will give me to do His will. The Word teaches me how to pray—with a strong desire, a firm faith, and constant perseverance. The Word teaches me not only who I am but who I may become. Above all it reminds me that Christ is the great intercessor and allows me to pray in His name.

Learn to renew your strength each day in God's Word and to pray according to His will.

Dear Father, I pray that when I read Your Word I may understand it. May the Holy Spirit teach me to know and use the Bible correctly, and may I see in it that Christ is all in all and will be all in me. May my prayers be consistent with what You have said in Your Word. In Jesus' name, amen.

OBEDIENCE

"If you obey me and do whatever I command you. . .
I will be your God."

JEREMIAH 11:4

God gave this command to Israel when He gave them the law, but Israel had no power to keep the law. So God gave a "new covenant" to enable His people to live a life of obedience. We read in Jeremiah 32:40: "I will make an everlasting covenant with them. . . . I will put a desire in their hearts to worship me, and they will never leave me." Ezekiel 36:27 says: "I will put my Spirit in you so you will obey my laws and do whatever I command." These wonderful promises gave the assurance that obedience would be their desire.

Listen to what Jesus says about obedience in John 14:21, 23: "Those who obey my commandments are the ones who love me. And because they love me, my Father will love them, and I will love them. . .and we will come to them and live with them."

No father can train his children unless they are obedient. No teacher can teach a child who continues to disobey him. No general can lead his soldiers to victory without prompt obedience. Ask God to imprint this lesson on your heart: The life of faith is a life of obedience. As Christ lived in obedience to the Father, so we need to live in loving obedience to God.

Do you think it's impossible for you to be obedient? It may be impossible to you, but not to God. He has promised to "put My Spirit in you so you will obey My laws." Pray and meditate on these words.

Holy Spirit, please give me power to do God's will. Let my fellowship with the Father and with the Lord Jesus Christ have quiet, unquestioning obedience as its one aim and object. Amen.

CONFESSION OF SIN

If we confess our sins to him,
he is faithful and just to forgive us
and to cleanse us from every wrong.

1 JOHN 1:9

Too often the confession of sin is superficial and neglected. Few Christians realize how absolutely necessary confession is. An honest confession of sin gives power to live a life of victory over sin. We need to confess with a sincere heart every sin that may be a hindrance in our Christian lives.

Listen to what David says, "I confessed all my sins to you and stopped trying to hide them. I said to myself, 'I will confess my rebellion to the LORD.' And you forgave me! All my guilt is gone. . . . For you are my hiding place; you protect me from trouble. You surround me with songs of victory" (Psalm 32:5, 7). David speaks of a time when he was unwilling to confess his sin. "When I refused to confess my sin, I was weak and miserable" (verse 3). But when he had confessed his sin, a wonderful change came.

Confession means not only that I confess my sin with shame and repentance, but that I turn it over to God, trusting Him to take it away. Such confession implies that I am unable to get rid of my guilt unless, by an act of faith, I trust God to deliver me. This deliverance means that I know my sins are forgiven and that Christ undertakes to cleanse me from the sin and keep me from its power.

Dear Father, I commit myself to confess each sin, knowing that You will grant forgiveness and give me deliverance. Thank You that my burden of sin is taken by Jesus. In His name, amen.

THE FIRST LOVE

But I have this complaint against you.
You don't love me or each other as you did at first!

REVELATION 2:4

In Revelation 2:2–3, eight signs are mentioned showing the zeal of the church at Ephesus, but there was one bad sign. The Lord said: "Turn back to me again and work as you did at first. If you don't, I will come and remove your lampstand from its place among the churches" (verse 5). What was this sin? "You don't love me or each other as you did at first!" (verse 4).

We find the same sin in the church today. There is enthusiasm for the truth, there is continuous hard work, but what the Lord values most is missing: tender, fervent love for Him.

A Christian may be a good example in all he does, yet the tender love for Jesus is missing. There is no personal, daily fellowship with Christ. All the many activities with which people satisfy themselves are nothing in the eyes of the Master.

Dear friend, this book speaks of the fellowship of love with Christ and spending time in His presence. Everything depends on this. Christ came from heaven to love us just as the Father loved Him. He suffered to win our hearts for this love. His love can be satisfied with nothing less than deep personal love.

Christ considers this of prime importance. Let us do so, too. Even though we are doing many good things "for the Lord," we must not leave "our first love."

Father, please help me make the love of Jesus my all—in my work and in my daily life. Amen.

THE HOLY SPIRIT

He will bring me glory by revealing to you
whatever he receives from me.

JOHN 16:14

The last night that He was with His disciples, Jesus promised to send the Holy Spirit as a Comforter. Although His bodily presence was removed, they would realize His presence in them and with them in a wonderful way. The Holy Spirit of God would reveal Christ in their hearts so that they would experience His presence with them continually. The Spirit would glorify Christ and would reveal to them the glorified Christ in love and power.

Do not fail to understand, to believe, and to experience this wonderful truth. Doing the Lord's work is not a duty performed in one's own strength. No, that is impossible; it is the Holy Spirit alone who will teach us to love Him sincerely.

God must have entire possession of us. He claims our whole heart and life. He will give us the strength to have fellowship with Christ, to keep His commandments, and to abide in His love. Once we have grasped this truth, we will begin to feel our deep dependence on the Holy Spirit and ask the Father to send Him in power into our hearts.

Lord, teach me to love the Word, to meditate on it, and to keep it. Reveal the love of Christ to me that I may love Him with a pure heart. In His name, amen.

CHRIST'S LOVE TO US

"I have loved you even as the Father has loved me.
Remain in my love."

JOHN 15:9

In relationships between friends and relatives, everything depends on their love to each other. What value is wealth if love is lacking between husband and wife, or parents and children? What value is knowledge and enthusiasm in God's work without the knowledge and experience of Christ's love? (See 1 Corinthians 13:1–3.) Christians need to know by experience how much Christ loves them, and to learn how they may abide and continue in that love.

Christ says: "As the Father has loved Me"—that is a divine, everlasting, wonderful love! "I also have loved you." The same love with which He had loved the Father He now gives us. He really desires that this everlasting love should rest upon us. What a blessing! Christ wants us to live in the power of the love of God that He also experienced.

In your fellowship with Christ in private or in public, you are surrounded by God's love. Jesus longs to fill you with His love.

Read from time to time what God's Word says about the love of Christ. Meditate on the words and let them sink into your heart. Sooner or later you will begin to realize: The greatest happiness of your life is that you are loved by the Lord Jesus and can live in fellowship with Him every day.

Lord Jesus, Your love to me is beyond words. I long to continue abiding in Your love. Amen.

OUR LOVE TO CHRIST

You love him even though you have never seen him.
Though you do not see him, you trust him.

1 PETER 1:8

People who had never seen Christ still truly loved Him and believed on Him. Their hearts were filled with unspeakable joy. Such is the life of a Christian who really loves the Lord.

The chief attribute of the Father and of the Son is love to each other and love to man. This should be the chief characteristic of the true Christian. Life becomes a well of living water, flowing out as love to the Lord Jesus.

This love is not merely a happy feeling. It is an active principle. It takes pleasure in doing the will of the Lord. It is joy to keep His commandments. As the love of Christ was shown to us by His death on the cross, our love must be exhibited in unselfish, self-sacrificing lives. Please understand this: In the Christian life, love to Christ is everything!

Great love results in great faith—faith in His love to us, faith in the powerful revelation of His love in our hearts, faith that He will work all His good pleasure in us. The wings of faith and love will lift us up to heaven and we shall be filled with joy beyond words. The joy of the Christian is an indispensable witness to the world of the power of Christ to change hearts and to fill them with love and gladness.

Take time daily in His presence to drink in His love.

Lord, make me strong in faith that my joy will be full. Let love, joy, and faith be my life each day through the grace of the Lord Jesus. Amen.

LOVE TO CHRISTIANS

"So now I am giving you a new commandment:
Love each other."

JOHN 13:34

Jesus told His disciples that as the Father had loved Him, even so He loved them. And now, following His example, we must love one another with the same love. "Your love for one another will prove to the world that you are my disciples" (John 13:35). He had prayed: "My prayer for all of them is that they will be one, just as you and I are one, Father—that just as you are in me and I am in you, so they will be in us, and the world will believe you sent me" (John 17:21). If we exhibit the love that was in God towards Christ, and in Christ to us, the world will be obliged to confess that our Christianity is genuine.

This is what actually happened. The Greeks and Romans, Jews and heathen, hated each other. Between all the nations of the world there was hardly a thought of love. The very idea of self-sacrifice was a strange one. When unbelievers saw that Christians from different nations, under the powerful working of the Holy Spirit, loved one another even to the point of self-sacrifice in times of need—they were amazed. They said: "Behold how these people love one another!"

Often Christ's love is not evident among Christians. Ask God to enable you to love your fellow believers as Christ loves you.

Father, may I abide in Christ's love and let that love fill my heart. As close as the bond of love is between You and Jesus, so close may my love be with all Your children. In Jesus' name, amen.

LOVE TO SINNERS

You can be sure that the one who brings that person back will save that sinner from death.

JAMES 5:20

What a wonderful thought—that I may save a sinner from everlasting death. This can happen if I bring that person back to the truth. This is the calling of every Christian.

When Christ and His love took possession of our hearts, He gave us this love that we might bring others to Him. This is how Christ's Kingdom is extended. Everyone who has the love of Christ is constrained to tell others. In the early Christian Church people went out and shared the love of Christ. Secular writers have told us that the rapid spread of Christianity in the first century was because each convert tried to bring the good news to others.

What a change has come over the Church! Many Christians never try to bring others to Christ. May the time soon come when Christians will feel constrained to share the love of Christ.

In a revival in Korea the converts were filled with such a burning love for Christ that they felt bound to tell others of His love. It was even taken as a test of membership that each one should have brought another to the Lord before being admitted to the church.

Lord Jesus, help me to think not only of my own life but also of the life of others. Having received the gift of God's love, may I pass it on to others. May I know the joy of bringing sinners to You. Amen.

THE SPIRIT OF LOVE

For we know how dearly God loves us, because he has given us the Holy Spirit to fill our hearts with his love.

ROMANS 5:5

I s it impossible for a Christian to live this life of love? Often we make little progress in this spirit of love because of our unbelief and lack of faith in God's promises.

We need continually to remind ourselves that it is not in our own strength that we can reach the love of Christ. The love of God is shed abroad in our hearts daily by the Spirit of God. It is only as we are wholly surrendered to the Spirit that we will be able to live according to God's will. When the inner life of love is renewed from day to day, we shall love others.

You can pray with Paul: "When I think of the wisdom and scope of God's plan, I fall to my knees and pray to the Father. . . that from his glorious, unlimited resources he will give you mighty inner strength through his Holy Spirit. And I pray that Christ will be more and more at home in your hearts as you trust in him. May your roots go down deep into the soil of God's marvelous love. And may you have the power to understand, as all God's people should, how wide, how long, how high, and how deep his love really is" (Ephesians 3:14–18). You may know this love on one condition: You must be strengthened by the Spirit so that Christ may dwell in your heart.

Take this message from God's Word. Unless you are on your knees you cannot live in this love. A life of prayer will make a life of love to Christ, other Christians, and those without Christ a reality in your experience.

I bow my knees unto You, Father. Strengthen me by Your Spirit so that Christ may dwell in my heart. May I be rooted and grounded in the love of Christ. In His name, amen.

PERSEVERING PRAYER

Keep on praying.

1 THESSALONIANS 5:17

O ne of the greatest drawbacks to the life of prayer is that the answer does not come as quickly as we expect. We are discouraged and think: "Perhaps I do not pray right." So we do not persevere. Jesus often talked about this. There may be a reason for the delay and the waiting may bring a blessing. Our desire must grow deeper and stronger, and we must ask with our whole heart. God puts us into the practicing school of persevering prayer so that our weak faith may be strengthened.

Above all, God wants to draw us into closer fellowship with Him. When our prayers are not answered we learn that the fellowship and love of God are more to us than the answers of our requests, and then we continue in prayer.

Do not be not impatient or discouraged if the answer does not come. "Always be prayerful." "Keep on praying." You will find real blessing in doing so. Ask whether your prayer is really in accordance with the will of God and the Word of God. Ask if it is in the right spirit and in the name of Christ. You will learn that the delay in the answer is one of the most precious ways God gives you His grace.

Those who have persevered before God are those who have had the greatest power in prayer.

Dear Jesus, help me to learn to persevere in prayer. Teach me through delayed answers to learn more of You and how You want me to pray. Amen.

THE PRAYER MEETING

They all met together continually for prayer. . . .
And everyone present was filled with the Holy Spirit.

ACTS 1:14; 2:4 (SEE ALSO MATTHEW 18:19–20)

I n a genuine prayer meeting God's children meet together, not as in church to listen to one speaker, but to lift up their hearts unitedly to God. Christians are drawn closer to each other. Those who are weak are strengthened and encouraged by the testimony of the older and more experienced members, and young Christians have the opportunity of telling of the joy of the Lord. As a result, God's blessing is poured out at home and abroad.

But there are also dangers to be considered. Some may attend and be edified but never learn to pray themselves. Others go for the religious fervor, and have a form of godliness, but do not know the hidden life of prayer. Unless there is much prayer alone in the presence of God, attendance at a prayer meeting may be a mere ritual.

A "living prayer" meeting will have great influence when its roots are nourished by the life of prayer alone in God's presence. Prayer should include God's people all over the world. As on the Day of Pentecost, there must be waiting on God for the filling of the Holy Spirit.

Remember, you do not live for yourself alone but are part of the Body of Christ. As the roots of the tree hidden deep in the earth and the branches that spread out to heaven are one, so the hidden prayer life is inseparably bound up with united prayer.

Father, may my participation in prayer meetings be much more than a form of social activity. Give me the joy of experiencing united prayer that moves heaven and earth. In Jesus' name, amen.

INTERCESSION

*Pray at all times and on every occasion
in the power of the Holy Spirit.*

EPHESIANS 6:18

W ill God really make the pouring out of blessing on others dependent on our prayers? Yes, He makes us His fellow workers. He has taken us into partnership in His work. If we fail to do our part, others will suffer and His work will suffer.

God has appointed intercession as one of the means by which others will be saved and Christians built up in the faith. People all over the world will receive life and blessing through our prayers. Should we not expect God's children to endeavor with all our strength to pray for God's blessing on the world?

Begin to use intercession as a means of grace for yourself and for others. Pray for your neighbors. Pray for sinners that they may come to Christ. Pray for your minister and for missionaries. Pray for your country and for government leaders. If you live a life completely for God, you will realize that the time spent in prayer is an offering pleasing to God.

Yes, "pray at all times. . .and be persistent in your prayers for all Christians everywhere." In so doing you will learn the lesson that intercession is the chief means of bringing others to Christ and bringing glory to God.

Lord Jesus, I pray for my neighbors and for those where I work, that they will come to know You. I pray for our pastor and for all who minister the gospel. And I pray for our country and its leaders, that we may put our trust in You. In Jesus' name, amen.

PRAYER AND FASTING

Jesus told them. . .
"But this kind of demon won't leave unless
you have prayed and fasted."

MATTHEW 17:20–21

J esus teaches us that a life of faith requires both prayer and fasting. Prayer grasps the power of heaven, fasting loosens the hold on earthly pleasure.

Jesus Himself fasted to get strength to resist the devil. He taught His disciples that fasting should be in secret, and the Father would reward it openly. Abstinence from food, or moderation in taking it, helps to focus on communication with God.

Let's remember that abstinence, moderation, and self-denial are a help to the spiritual life. After having eaten a hearty meal, one does not feel much desire to pray. To willingly sacrifice our own pleasure or enjoyment will help to focus our minds more fully on God and His priorities. The very practice needed in overcoming our own desires will give us strength to take hold of God in prayer.

Our lack of discipline in prayer comes from our fleshly desire of comfort and ease. "Those who belong to Christ Jesus have nailed the passions and desires of their sinful nature to his cross and crucified them there" (Galatians 5:24). Prayer is not easy work. For the real practice of prayer—taking hold of God and having communion and fellowship with Him—it is necessary that our selfish desires be sacrificed.

Isn't it worth the trouble to deny ourselves daily in order to meet the holy God and receive His blessings?

Heavenly Father, help me to joyfully give up earthly pleasures and the desires of the flesh so that my prayers may be more powerful and effective. In Jesus' name, amen.

THE SPIRIT OF PRAYER

*For the Spirit pleads for us believers
in harmony with God's own will.*

ROMANS 8:27

Prayer is not our work. It is God's work in us by His almighty power. As we pray, our attitude should be one of silent expectation that the Holy Spirit will help in our weakness and pray for us with groanings that cannot be expressed.

What a thought! When I feel how imperfect my prayer is, when I have no strength of my own, I may bow in silence before God in the confidence that His Holy Spirit will teach me to pray. The Spirit is the Spirit of prayer. It is not my work, but God's work in me. The Spirit will make perfect the work even in my weakness.

We see an example of this in the story of Jacob. The same One who wrestled with him and seemed to withhold the blessing was in reality strengthening him to continue and to prevail in prayer. Prayer is the work of the Triune God: the Father, who gives the desire and will provide all we need; the Son, who through His intercession teaches us to pray in His name; and the Holy Spirit, who in secret will strengthen our weak desires.

The Spirit of truth will glorify Christ in us, and the Spirit of love will shed this love abroad in our hearts. And we have the Spirit of prayer, through whom our life may be one of continual prayer. Thank God that the Holy Spirit has been given to teach us to pray.

Holy Spirit, I desire to listen to Your leading. Help me to obey Your voice in all things. Make me a person of prayer. In Jesus' name, amen.

WHOLLY FOR CHRIST

Christ died for everyone. . .
so that those who receive his new life
will no longer live to please themselves.

2 CORINTHIANS 5:14–15

Paul describes here a threefold life. First, the life of the Christian who lives according to his old nature: for himself alone. The second, the life of the true Christian: he lives wholly for Christ. Third, the life of Christ in heaven: He lives wholly for us.

We need to be convinced of the foolishness of living only for ourselves. At conversion we focus more on our own salvation and less on the claim that Christ has on us. Many Christians continue to live for themselves, content with doing little for the Master. Happiness comes to the believer who realizes the privilege of consecrating one's life entirely to God.

The great hindrance to such a life is the unbelief which says it is impossible. But when the truth takes hold—Christ in heaven lives for me and will impart His life to me—then we know that He will enable us to live wholly for Him.

May this be your earnest desire, your prayer, and your firm expectation: Christ has not only died for me but lives in heaven to keep me, His purchased possession. Christ will keep you as a member of His Body, to work and live for Him. Pray for grace to live completely for God, whether in sharing with unbelievers or in serving His people. Take time to be united with Christ in prayer so that you can say with all your heart: I live wholly for Him.

Dear Lord Jesus, from this moment let my prayer each day be: Wholly for Christ. Amen.

THE CROSS OF CHRIST

I have been crucified with Christ.

GALATIANS 2:19

The cross of Christ is His greatest glory. Because He humbled Himself by dying on the cross in our place, therefore God has highly exalted Him. The cross was the power that conquered Satan and sin.

As Christians we share with Christ in the cross. Christ lives in us through the Holy Spirit, and we live as one who has died with Christ. As we realize the power of Christ's crucifixion, we live as one who has died to the world and to sin. Christ, the crucified One, lives in us.

Jesus said to His disciples: "If any of you wants to be my follower. . .you must put aside your selfish ambition, shoulder your cross, and follow me" (Mark 8:34). They had seen men carrying a cross. They knew that it meant a painful death. All His life Christ bore His cross—the death sentence that He should die for the world. As Christians we must bear the cross, acknowledging that we are worthy of death, believing that we are crucified with Christ, and that the crucified One lives in us. "Our old sinful selves were crucified with Christ" (Romans 6:6). "Those who belong to Christ Jesus have nailed the passions and desires of their sinful nature to his cross and crucified them there" (Galatians 5:24). When we have accepted this life of the cross, we will be able to say: "God forbid that I should boast about anything except the cross of our Lord Jesus Christ" (Galatians 6:14).

Allow the Holy Spirit to teach you more about this deep spiritual truth.

Lord, may I remember Your sacrifice and Your self-denial. May the power of Your death work in me. Help me become like You in Your death so that I will know the power of Your resurrection. Amen.

THE WORLD

When you love the world,
you show that you do not have the love of the Father in you.

1 JOHN 2:15

John teaches us what he means by the world in 1 John 2:16. He says: "For the world offers only the lust for physical pleasure, the lust for everything we see, and pride in our possessions. These are not from the Father. They are from this evil world."

Because all mankind has fallen through sin, we have come under the power of the world and are deceived by the god of this world. The world with its pleasures surrounds the Christian each day with temptations.

This was the case with Eve in the Garden of Eden. We find in Genesis the three characteristics John mentions: (1) The lust of the flesh—"The woman saw that the tree was good for food." (2) The lust of the eyes—"It was pleasant to the eyes." (3) The pride of life—"A tree to be desired to make one wise" (Genesis 3:6 KJV). Our life in the world is full of danger—so much to occupy our eyes and our hearts, so much worldly wisdom and knowledge.

So John tells us: "Stop loving this evil world and all that it offers you, for when you love the world, you show that you do not have the love of the Father in you." Just as the Lord called His disciples, He calls us to leave all and follow Him.

Lord Jesus, in this dangerous world, help me to be wholly devoted to You. I look forward to my daily fellowship with You. Amen.

PUT ON CHRIST

For as many of you as have been
baptized into Christ have put on Christ.

GALATIANS 3:27 KJV

The word that is here translated "put on" is the same that is used in regard to putting on clothes. We have put on "the new man," and we have the new nature as a garment that is worn so all can see who we are. The Christian is known as one who has put on Christ and exhibits Him in his whole life and character.

Paul says to "put on the Lord Jesus," not only at conversion, but from day to day. As you put on your clothes each day, so the Christian must daily put on the Lord Jesus. In that way you reflect the image of Jesus, the new person formed in His likeness.

Put on Christ! This must be done by spending time alone in His presence. As my clothes protect me from wind and sun, even so Christ will be my protection and my joy. As I fellowship with Him in prayer, He strengthens me.

Take time to meditate on this wonderful truth. As your clothing is a necessity, let it be equally indispensable for you to "put on" Jesus Christ, to spend time with Him, and to walk with Him all the day. Take the time and the trouble to do this. Your reward will be great.

Father, I choose to put on Christ and to demonstrate His life in me. Help me to live out my commitment. In Jesus' name, amen.

THE STRENGTH OF THE CHRISTIAN

A final word:
Be strong with the Lord's mighty power.

EPHESIANS 6:10

Since we as Christians have no strength of our own, where may we get it? Notice the answer: Be strong with the Lord's mighty power.

Paul had spoken of this power in the earlier part of Ephesians (1:17–20). He had prayed to God to give them the Spirit that they might know the greatness of His power which He displayed when He raised Christ from the dead. This is the literal truth: The greatness of His power which raised Christ from the dead works in every believer. We hardly believe it and much less experience it. That is why Paul prays that God would teach us to believe in His almighty power.

In Ephesians 3:16–17, Paul asks the Father to strengthen them by His Spirit, that Christ might dwell in their hearts. And then in verse 20: "Now glory be to God! By his mighty power at work within us, he is able to accomplish infinitely more than we would ever dare to ask or hope."

Read over these Scriptures again and pray for God's Spirit to make these words real to you. Believe in the divine power working in you. Pray that the Holy Spirit may reveal it to you. Appropriate the promise that God will show His power in your heart, supplying all your needs. It is clear that much time is needed with the Father and the Son, if you would experience the power of God within you.

Father, grant me the Spirit of wisdom that I may experience this wonderful power in my life. I ask in Jesus' name, amen.

THE WHOLE HEART

With my whole heart have I sought thee.

PSALM 119:10 KJV

Notice how often the psalmist speaks of the "all the heart" or the "whole heart": "Search for him with all their hearts" (verse 2); "I will put it into practice with all my heart" (verse 34); "I obey your commandments with all my heart" (verse 69); "I pray with all my heart" (verse 145). In seeking God, in observing His law, in crying for His help—each time it is with his whole heart.

When we want to be successful in business, we put our whole heart into it. Isn't this even more necessary in the service of a holy God? He is worthy. The whole heart is needed in the service of God when we worship Him.

We often forget this. In prayer, in reading His word, in seeking to do His will, we fail to say continually: "I have tried my best—with my whole heart—to find You." Let us learn to say: "I desire to seek God and to serve Him with my whole heart."

Meditate and pray about this. Spend time before God until you know that you really mean what you say and you have the assurance that God will hear your prayer. Then each morning as you approach God in prayer you can honestly say, "I seek You with my whole heart." You gradually will feel the need of waiting in holy stillness upon God so that He may take possession of your whole heart. You will learn to love Him with your whole heart and your whole mind.

Dear Lord, I desire to know You with my whole heart. May my every act of worship, my prayer, my time in Your Word, all be wholehearted. In Jesus' name, amen.

A BLESSED REALITY

God alone made it possible for you to be in Christ Jesus.

1 CORINTHIANS 1:30

During His last day with His disciples, the Lord Jesus made several references to being "in Christ Jesus." "When I am raised to life again, you will know that I am in my Father, and you are in me, and I am in you" (John 14:20). Following that is 15:5: "Those who remain in me, and I in them, will produce much fruit." "If you stay joined to me and my words remain in you, you may ask any request you like, and it will be granted!" (15:7). We cannot apply these promises unless we first prayerfully accept the words "in Christ."

Paul expressed the same thought in Romans 6:4: "We. . . were buried with Christ." "You should consider yourselves dead to sin and able to live for the glory of God through Christ Jesus" (Romans 6:11). "There is no condemnation for those who belong to Christ Jesus" (Romans 8:1). And in Ephesians 1:3: "How we praise God. . .who has blessed us with every spiritual blessing in the heavenly realms because we belong to Christ." Colossians 2:9: "For in Christ the fullness of God lives in a human body." Colossians 2:6: "Just as you accepted Christ Jesus as your Lord, you must continue to live in obedience to him." Colossians 4:12: "Asking God to make you strong and perfect, fully confident of the whole will of God."

By faith take hold of the truth that "God establishes us in Christ" and then follow the leading of the Spirit in prayer.

Dear God, may Your Word take root in my heart so that I will realize something of its power. I desire to spend time each day in fellowship with Christ until abiding in Him becomes a reality. In His name I pray, amen.

CHRIST IN ME

Examine yourselves to see if your faith is really genuine.

2 CORINTHIANS 13:5

C hrist is in me. What a difference it would make if we could take time every morning to focus on the thought: Christ is in me.

Christ made it clear to His disciples. The Spirit would teach them: "When I am raised to life again, you will know that I am in my Father, and you are in me, and I am in you" (John 14:20). Through the power of God we who believe were crucified with Christ and raised again with Him. As a result Christ is in us! Through faith in God's Word, the Christian accepts it.

Paul expresses this thought in the prayer of Ephesians 3:16: "I pray that from his glorious, unlimited resources he will give you mighty inner strength through his Holy Spirit." Notice that it is not the ordinary gift of grace, but a special revelation of the riches of His love that Christ may dwell in your heart by faith. Have you been able to grasp that?

Paul said: "I fall to my knees and pray to the Father" (Ephesians 3:14). That is the only way to obtain the blessing. Take time in prayer in His presence to realize: "Christ dwells in me." Even in the midst of your daily schedule, look upon your heart as the dwelling place of the Son of God. Then Christ's words, "Those who remain in me, and I in them, will produce much fruit" (John 15:5), will become your daily experience.

Father, today as I come quietly before You in secret, help me to experience the wonderful reality of Christ in me. Amen.

CHRIST IS ALL

Christ is all that matters, and he lives in all of us.

COLOSSIANS 3:11

C hrist is all—in the eternal counsel of God, in the redemption on the cross, as King on the throne in heaven and on earth. In the salvation of sinners, in the building up of Christ's Body, in the care for individuals—Christ is all. Every hour and every day this knowledge provides comfort and strength to the child of God.

You feel too weak, too unworthy, too untrustworthy. But if you will only accept the Lord Jesus in childlike faith, you have a guide who will supply all your need. Believe the word of our Savior in Matthew 28:20: "And be sure of this: I am with you always," and you will experience His presence each day.

However cold and dull your feelings may be, however sinful you are, meet the Lord Jesus in secret and He will reveal Himself to you. Tell Him how miserable you really are, and then trust Him to help and sustain you.

Each day as you spend time in His presence, let this thought be with you: Christ is all. Make it your goal: Christ is all—to teach me to pray, to strengthen my faith, to give me the assurance of His love, to give me direct access to the Father, to make me strong for the schedule of the day.

Lord Jesus Christ, You are all I need. Teach me to abide in Your love so I will have the assurance that You dwell in my heart. May I know the love that passes knowledge. Praise God: You, Christ, are my all in all! Amen.

THE LOVE OF GOD

God is love,
and all who live in love live in God,
and God lives in them.

1 JOHN 4:16

The love of God—what an unfathomable mystery! Jesus said: "Only God is good" (Matthew 19:17). The glory of God in heaven is that He wills to do all that is good. That includes the two meanings of the word: good—all that is right and perfect; good—all that makes happy.

The God who wills nothing but good is a God of love. He does not demand His own way. He does not live for Himself but pours out His love on all living creatures. All created things share in this love so that they may be satisfied with that which is good.

A characteristic of love is that it "does not demand its own way" (1 Corinthians 13:5). It finds happiness in giving to others. It sacrifices itself wholly for others. God offered Himself to mankind in love in the person of His Son, and the Son offered Himself upon the cross to bring that love to men and women. The everlasting love with which the Father loved the Son is the same love with which the Son loves us.

The love of God to His Son, the love of the Son to us, the love with which we love the Son, the love with which we love each other and try to love all men—all is the same eternal, incomprehensible, almighty love of God. Love is the power of the Godhead in the Father, Son, and Holy Spirit.

God of love, thank You for loving me the way You do. It is beyond my understanding. I praise You for Your love. Amen.

THE LOVE OF CHRIST

Whatever we do, it is because Christ's love controls us.

2 CORINTHIANS 5:14

God sent His Son into the world to let us know His ever-lasting love, even as it was known in heaven. Even the angels in heaven are filled with praise and worship because of God's love. God's desire is that on this sinful earth His love would take possession of the hearts of men and women.

In order to reveal His love and win our hearts to Himself, God sent Christ, the Son of His love, to earth. The Lord Jesus Christ became man and, even though He was God, humbly made Himself nothing. In His dealings with the poor, the unbelieving, and the rebellious—and through His miracles—He poured out His love into the hearts of sinful men.

God gave the greatest proof of love that the world has ever seen. On the cross He took our sins upon Himself. He bore the suffering and the scorn of His enemies so that friend and foe alike might know God's eternal love.

Then, after He had ascended to heaven, He gave the Holy Spirit to shed abroad this love in our hearts. Impelled by the love of Christ, the disciples in turn offered their lives to make this love known to others.

Think about this. God longs to have our hearts filled with His love so that He can use us as channels for this love to flow out to others. Let us be satisfied with nothing less and sacrifice everything to secure a place for this love in the hearts of men and women.

Father, thank You for paying such a price so that I can share in Your love. Help me to share it with others. In Jesus' name, amen.

THE LOVE OF THE SPIRIT

He has given us the Holy Spirit to fill our hearts with his love.

ROMANS 5:5

As God's children, we must confess that we know very little of fervent, childlike love for our heavenly Father. Why is this? Perhaps we have not learned the lesson that there must be a constant renewal of faith in what God is able to do. We try to stir up love towards God in our hearts. Yet, in our own strength, we cannot awaken the slightest love to God.

Child of God, believe that the love of God will work as the power in your heart that enables you to love God and to love others. Cease to expect love in yourself. Believe in the power of God's love resting on you and teaching you to love God with His own love.

Learn the lesson of our text: "He has given us the Holy Spirit to fill our hearts with his love." The Spirit will enable us to love God, our friends, and even our enemies. Be assured of two things. First, in your own strength you cannot love God or your fellow Christians. And second, the Holy Spirit is within you every day and every hour, seeking to fill you with the Spirit of love. Each morning as you commit yourself into the keeping of the Holy Spirit, let this prayer arise:

Lord, grant me the assurance that You will pour forth the love of Christ into my own heart, and then let it stream forth to all around me! Amen.

THE POWER OF LOVE

Overwhelming victory is ours through Christ,
who loved us.

ROMANS 8:37

In days of uncertainty, strong racial feelings, and unrest, we need to experience the love of God. Let us anchor our hope in the truth, "God is love." God's power, by which He rules the world, is the power of undying love. He works through the hearts and wills of men and women who are wholly yielded to Him. He waits for us to open our hearts to Him in love. Then, full of courage, we become witnesses for Him.

This is how Christ's kingdom is manifested and His reign of love on earth began. Christ died in order to establish this kingdom. The only means He used to gain influence was by showing a serving, suffering love. He saw the possibility of redemption in even the worst of people, knowing that their hearts could never resist the steady influence of love. It was in the fervor of that love that Jesus' disciples were able to do the impossible.

The spirit of hatred and bitterness can never be overcome by argument or reproaches. Some think things can never be different, but if we really believe in the omnipotence of God's love, we may trust His power. Our faith in love as the greatest power in the world should prepare us for a life in communion with God in prayer and for a life of service.

Lord, give me grace as I examine how I am living my life. Enable me, as a servant of Your love, to live for those around me. In Jesus' name, amen.

THE SIGN OF A TRUE CHURCH

*Your love for one another will prove to the world
that you are my disciples.*

JOHN 13:35

W e are taught in most of our creeds that the true church is to be found where God's Word is faithfully and accurately preached and the sacraments are dispensed as instituted by Christ. Christ Himself takes a much broader view. To Him the distinguishing mark of His followers is not merely what the Church teaches—but how we live our lives showing love to each other.

Jesus' death on the cross was love at its highest. We owe everything to this love. Love is the power that moved Christ to die for us. In love, God highly exalted Him as Lord and Christ. Love is the power that broke our hearts, and love is the power that heals them. Love is the power through which Christ dwells and works in us. Love can change my nature and enable me to surrender to God. It gives me strength to live a holy, joyous life, full of blessing to others. Every Christian should show the love of God.

Many Christians are sure it is impossible to lead such a life, and they do not even greatly desire it. They do not understand that we may and can love with God's own love.

If we fully believe that the Holy Spirit, dwelling within us, will maintain this heavenly love from hour to hour, we will be able to understand the words of Christ: "Anything is possible if a person believes" (Mark 9:23). Then we will be able to love God with all our hearts, to love family and friends, and even our enemies.

Holy Spirit, I am totally dependent upon You if I am to live a life that shows forth the love of God. Please fill me and enable me to live such a life. In Jesus' name, amen.

RACE-HATRED

Once we, too, were foolish and disobedient.
We were misled by others and became slaves to
many wicked desires and evil pleasures.

TITUS 3:3

O ur text paints a dark picture of the state of human nature! What causes such a sad condition? The answer is "Adam's fall." Think how Cain, the first child born of the man God created, shed the blood of his brother Abel. The first child born on earth came under the power of the devil, who "was a murderer from the beginning" (John 8:44). "Now the LORD observed the extent of the people's wickedness, and he saw that all their thoughts were consistently and totally evil" (Genesis 6:5). No wonder He destroyed mankind by a flood.

Humanity's love of their own people, implanted in their hearts by nature, soon changed to hatred of other peoples. Love of country became the source of race-hatred and bloodshed. Note how God has placed the races side by side to see if our Christianity will enable us to overcome race-hatred. Will we, in the power of Christ's love, prove that "In this new life, it doesn't matter if you are a Jew or a Gentile, circumcised or uncircumcised, barbaric, uncivilized, slave, or free. Christ is all that matters, and he lives in all of us" (Colossians 3:11)?

What an opportunity there is for the Church to prove the power of God's love to change race-hatred into brotherly love! God has abundant power to make this happen. As Christians we need to pray for ourselves and for each other that we would obey the Word of God and live in the power of Christ's love.

O God, make known to us Your love in heavenly power, and let it take
full possession of our lives! May Your Church be an example of love for
all mankind. In Jesus' name, amen.

LOVE YOUR ENEMIES

You have heard that the law of Moses says,
"Love your neighbor" and hate your enemy.

MATTHEW 5:43

Religious teachers in Christ's day judged that they had a right to say this [Matthew 5:43] because of Leviticus 19:17–18: "Do not nurse hatred in your heart for any of your relatives. Confront your neighbors directly so you will not be held guilty for their crimes. Never seek revenge or bear a grudge against anyone, but love your neighbor as yourself." They argued that it was only their own people whom they may not hate; it was all right to hate their enemies. But our Lord said: "Love your enemies! Pray for those who persecute you!" (Matthew 5:44).

How often we as Christians follow the example of those religious leaders! The new commandment to love requires much grace, costs time, and needs much earnest prayer.

When I was a minister in Cape Town I met a German deaconess. She had a class for several Kaffirs who were preparing to join the church. One evening she spoke about loving our enemies. She asked one man if his people had enemies. "Oh yes!" "Who are they?" "The Fingoes." She asked if he could love a Fingo. His answer was decided. "I can't love Fingo." She told him that in that case he could not go to the Communion. He seemed very downcast. He was not received into the church with the others but continued to attend the class. Then one evening he appeared with a bright face and said, "I now love Fingo." He had prayed about it, God heard his prayer and enabled him to love his enemy.

There is only one way we can love our enemies: by the love of Christ, sought and found in prayer.

Father, help me by the power of Your Spirit to truly love my enemies. In Jesus' name, amen.

As God Forgives

And forgive us our sins—
just as we forgive those who have sinned against us.

LUKE 11:4

The forgiveness of sins is the one great gift that sets the sinner free. Forgiveness gives us boldness toward God and is the source of our salvation. The forgiveness of sins gives us a reason to be thankful every day of our lives.

As we walk with God in the assurance of sins forgiven, He desires that we should live as those who have been freely forgiven. We can only prove our sincerity by forgiving those who have offended us as willingly as God has forgiven us.

In the Lord's Prayer we are taught to pray: "Forgive us our sins—just as we forgive those who have sinned against us." Then at the end: "But if you refuse to forgive others, your Father will not forgive your sins" (Matthew 6:15). In Matthew 18:21 we have the question of Peter: "Lord, how often should I forgive someone who sins against me?" Our Lord answered, "Seventy times seven!"

Then follows the parable of the servant whose lord forgave him his debt but who would not show compassion on his fellow servant. His lord asked: "Shouldn't you have mercy on your fellow servant, just as I had mercy on you?" So the servant was sent to prison. The Lord warns us: "That's what my heavenly Father will do to you if you refuse to forgive your brothers and sisters in your heart" (Matthew 18:33, 35).

Lord, as I need Your forgiveness each day so let me be ready to forgive my brother. In Jesus' name, amen.

THE TWO LEADERS

I urge you, first of all, to pray for all people.
As you make your requests, plead for God's mercy upon them,
and give thanks.

1 TIMOTHY 2:1

At the time of the unveiling of the Women's Monument at Bloemfontein, South Africa, I spoke a few words about the suffering, praying, all-conquering love of these women. They prayed that God would help them love their enemies and keep them from hatred. I expressed the hope that the feeling of peace and unity might continue and this prayerful love be ours. I said that there were some who feared disunion, not only between the two races in the country, but between those who were of the same race. Not long after, we heard that there had been a breach between the leaders of the two parties.

I felt impelled to write an article on the question: "For whom do you pray?" Someone answered: "I pray for the man at the head of my party who, under God's guidance, has now become the leader of all South Africa." And another, "I pray especially for the man who has brought the interests of my people into the foreground." Would it not be sad if we came into God's presence divided into two camps praying one against the other? We must pray for both our leaders and for all who are in authority. As leaders of the people, their influence for good or evil is inexpressible. Their hearts are in God's hands, and He can turn them wherever He wills. Let us pray to God in all sincerity for our leaders, that God will grant what is good for the whole land.

Lord, the hearts of rulers are in Your hands; teach them to do Your will. In Jesus' name, amen.

LOVE AND PRAYER

Be earnest and disciplined in your prayers.
Most important of all, continue to show deep love for each other.

1 PETER 4:7–8

E arnest prayer and fervent love are closely linked. If we pray only for ourselves, we will not find it easy to be in the right attitude toward God. But when our hearts are filled with love for others, we will continue to pray for them, even for those with whom we do not agree.

Prayer holds an important place in the life of love; they are inseparably connected. If you want your love to increase, forget yourself and pray for God's children. If you want to increase in prayerfulness, spend time loving those around you, helping to bear their burdens.

There is a great need for earnest, powerful intercessors! God desires His children to present themselves each day before the throne of grace to pray down the power of the Spirit upon all believers. Unity is strength. Spiritual unity will help us to live unselfishly, wholly for God and others. Let us apply Peter's words to our lives—"earnest in prayer. . .showing deep love for each other."

As we meditate on love to those around us, we will be drawn into fellowship with God. This will come, not by reading or thinking, but by spending time with the Father and with the Lord Jesus through the Holy Spirit. Love leads to prayer—to believing prayer is given the love of God.

Father, may Your love overwhelm me. May I love You and Your church with all my heart. In Jesus' name, amen.

THE FIRST COMMANDMENT

The LORD your God will cleanse your heart. . .
so that you will love him with all your heart and soul.

DEUTERONOMY 30:6

G od greatly desires our love. It is the nature of all love to want to be acceptable and to be accepted. God longs to have the love of our whole heart.

How can we love God with all our heart and soul? In the same way that we receive salvation—through faith alone. Paul says, "I live my life in this earthly body by trusting in the Son of God, who loved me and gave himself for me" (Galatians 2:20). When we take time to wait upon God and remember how God sought to win our love through the gift of His Son, we shall realize that God has a strong longing for our love.

Our hearts are blind. It is easy to forget that God longs for the love of His child. Once we believe it, we will feel constrained to wait before God and ask Him to let His light shine into our hearts. As the sun gives us its light, God is a thousand times more willing to give us the light of His love.

As we wait silently before God, we become strong in the assurance of faith. God, who longs for our love, is almighty and will fill us with His love by the Holy Spirit.

Take time each day to love God and believe Him with firmer faith. God will work within us, granting the desire to love Him with our whole heart. He will enable us to prove our love by keeping His commandments.

O Lord, I bow before You. Fulfill my desire, which is also Your desire, that my heart may be filled with You. Amen.

Pray for Love

And may the Lord make your love grow and overflow to each other and to everyone else, just as our love overflows toward you.

1 Thessalonians 3:12

Paul gives us a powerful prayer in this text: that the Lord would make them abound in love toward each other, so that their hearts would be without blame. Without love, true holiness was impossible. Let us use this prayer often.

In 2 Thessalonians 3:5 we read: "May the Lord bring you into an ever deeper understanding of the love of God." That is what the Lord Jesus will do for us. As the Apostle makes love the chief thing, let us do the same.

"I want you to know how much I have agonized for you. . . . My goal is that [you] will be encouraged and knit together by strong ties of love. I want [you] to have full confidence because [you] have complete understanding of God's secret plan, which is Christ himself" (Colossians 2:1–2). Paul considers love indispensable for growth in the knowledge of God. God's love can only be experienced when Christians are knit together in love and live for others, not only for themselves.

Take time to meditate on these prayers of Paul. As the sun freely gives its light to the grass that it may grow, so God is more willing to give His love to us. As you pray and ponder these words, you will gain a strong assurance of what God is able to do for you. He will make you to abound in love and strengthen you to live before Him in holiness and love for others.

Lord, by Your great love, grant me a heart of love. May my love "overflow more and more, and. . .keep on growing in. . .knowledge and understanding" that I may be "filled with the fruit of. . .salvation— those good things that are produced in [my] life by Jesus Christ" (Philippians 1:9, 11). Amen.

A SONG OF LOVE

There are three things that will endure—
faith, hope, and love—
and the greatest of these is love.

1 CORINTHIANS 13:13

Today is wholly devoted to the praise of love. The first three verses of 1 Corinthians 13 speak of the absolute necessity of love as the chief thing in our religion. "If I could speak in any language in heaven or on earth. . .if I had the gift of prophecy. . . if I had the gift of faith so that I could speak to a mountain and make it move. . .if I gave everything I have to the poor and even sacrificed my body. . .but if I didn't love others" then, three times repeated, "I would only be making meaningless noise like a loud gong or a clanging cymbal. . .what good would I be? . . .I would be of no value whatsoever." If I have not love, I am of no value.

There are fifteen things said about love, but one sentence sums up its whole nature: "It does not demand its own way" (verse 5). And again: "Love will last forever" (verse 8). Prophecies, unknown languages, and knowledge shall vanish away. Even faith and hope shall be changed into sight. But love lasts forever.

"Love does not demand its own way." Think and pray about this. "Love will last forever." Consider all that means. "The greatest of these is love." Let this love rule in your life.

God is love. "God is love, and all who live in love live in God, and God lives in them" (1 John 4:16). Let your heart be filled with love so that, by God's almighty power, you may be a witness to the transforming power of love. Then you will be a blessing to all around you.

Lord, may I live each day in fellowship with the triune love of Father, Son, and Holy Spirit so that I learn the secret of how to love. In Jesus' name, amen.

LIKE CHRIST

I have given you an example to follow. Do as I have done to you.

JOHN 13:15

The love of Christ is the basis not only of our salvation but also of our daily life and conduct. Jesus clearly says: "Do as I have done to you." The love of Christ is my only hope of salvation. Walking in that love is the way to enjoy that salvation.

"We should please others. If we do what helps them, we will build them up in the Lord. . . . So accept each other just as Christ has accepted you; then God will be glorified" (Romans 15:2, 7). God will work within us to "accept each other just as Christ has accepted us."

"Follow God's example in everything you do, because you are his dear children. Live a life filled with love for others, following the example of Christ, who loved you and gave himself as a sacrifice to take away your sins" (Ephesians 5:1–2). Paul reminds us that love is everything. Christ loved us so much He died on the cross so we could be God's dear children. It follows that we should walk in love. Those who keep close to Christ will walk in love.

"Since God chose you to be the holy people whom he loves, you must clothe yourselves with tenderhearted mercy. . . . You must make allowance for each other's faults and forgive the person who offends you. Remember, the Lord forgave you, so you must forgive others. And the most important piece of clothing you must wear is love. Love is what binds us all together in perfect harmony" (Colossians 3:12–14). As we walk in fellowship with Him, we are given strength to be like Him!

O God, Father of love, Father of Christ, our Father, will You indeed strengthen us each day to love one another in Christ, even as He loved us! Amen.

THE POWER OF GOD'S WORD

The very words I have spoken to you are spirit and life.

JOHN 6:63

Frequently the question is asked: Why do God's children often fail to realize the great value and absolute necessity of loving each other? One answer is unbelief. Without faith there can be no thought of the power of love within us. True faith acknowledges God's loving care for us and His power to work wonders in our hearts.

It is necessary to be deeply convinced of our total inability to produce this love on our own. We must have a burning desire to receive this heavenly love into our hearts—a love that is holy and can conquer sin and unbelief. When we gain an insight into what God's Word is—a living power in our hearts—we will be filled with the love of God by the Holy Spirit, living and working within us.

Are we ready to acknowledge our deep sinfulness and yield our hearts unreservedly for this love to take possession of us? Are we ready to take time in God's presence in the confidence that His Word will work in us as a seed of new life? If so, then we will love Jesus and each other with a love like God's love for us.

Oh what love, Father, that You have shown to us. Help us to commit ourselves to a love for each other that reflects Your love for us. In Jesus' name, amen.

THE LOVE THAT SUFFERS

Live a life filled with love for others,
following the example of Christ,
who loved you and gave himself as
a sacrifice to take away your sins.

EPHESIANS 5:2

It is strange that love, which is the source of the greatest happiness, should also be the cause of the most intense suffering. Suffering always follows when love seeks to save the object of its love. It is only by suffering that love can gain its end and so attain the highest happiness.

Even the almighty power of God's love could not achieve its purpose without suffering. By suffering, Christ bore the sins of the whole world. Love in the midst of suffering manifested the greatest glory and attained its end perfectly.

Love worthy of the name manifests itself in a life of continual self-sacrifice. Love gives strength to endure, whatever the circumstances. Loving others may mean tears, heartache, and much persevering in prayer; but love overcomes all obstacles.

Do you long to know the love of Christ in all its fullness? Then yield yourself to Him. Think of yourself as a channel through which the highest love can reach its aim. Begin to suffer with and intercede for those around you. Eventually you will realize what this life of love is: to live wholly for the welfare and happiness of others.

Dear Lord, may I know the real fellowship of Your love. Teach me unreserved surrender, always seeking Your glory in the service of others. In Christ's name, amen.

THE LACK OF PRAYER

And yet the reason you don't have what you want
is that you don't ask God for it.

JAMES 4:2

Recently I attended several conventions at which prayer was often the subject of conversation. A businessman said that the spirit of intercession is what the Church of our day needs. Everywhere people confessed, "We pray too little!" Yet there seemed to be a fear that, because of pressure from work and the force of habit, it was almost impossible to hope for change. Such thinking can only hinder our own joy and our power in God's service.

Dr. Whyte of Edinburgh said that, as a young minister, he thought any time left over from pastoral visitation ought to be spent with his books. He wanted to feed his people with the very best he could prepare. But now he had learned that prayer was more important than study. He felt as if it were almost too late to regain what he had lost and urged us to pray more. What a solemn confession and warning: We pray too little!

Is the call of God for our time and attention more important than our work? If God is waiting to meet us and to give us power from heaven for His work, it is shortsighted to put other work in His place. If there is to be a significant experience of God's presence, there must be more definite and persevering prayer.

Lord God, stir up faith and inspire assurance that God by His Spirit
will enable us to pray as we should. I ask in Jesus' name, amen.

Time for Prayer

Yet no one calls on your name or pleads with you for mercy.

ISAIAH 64:7

At a ministerial meeting the superintendent of a large district said: "I rise in the morning and have half an hour with God. I am occupied all day with numerous engagements. Not many minutes elapse without my breathing a prayer for guidance. After work I speak to God of the day's work. But I know little of the intense prayer of which Scripture speaks."

There are earnest Christians who have just enough prayer to maintain their spiritual position but not enough to grow spiritually. Seeking to fight off temptation is a defensive attitude rather than an assertive one which reaches for higher attainment. The scriptural teaching to cry out day and night in prayer must, to some degree, become our experience if we are to be intercessors.

A man said to me, "I see the importance of much prayer, and yet my life hardly allows time for it. Am I to give up? How can I accomplish what I desire?"

I admitted that the difficulty was universal and quoted a Dutch proverb: "What is heaviest must weigh heaviest." The most important must have the first place. The law of God is unchangeable. In our communication with heaven, we only get as we give. Unless we are willing to pay the price—to sacrifice time and attention and seemingly necessary tasks for the sake of the heavenly gifts—we cannot expect much power from heaven in our work.

Father, I see that I am not alone. If others with time pressure can learn to pray as they should, then I can also. Teach me to pray. In Jesus' name, amen.

FINDING THE ROOT CAUSE

And God will generously provide all you need.
Then you will always have everything you need
and plenty left over to share with others.

2 CORINTHIANS 9:8

I met a clergyman who used the expression "the distraction of business." It was one of the greatest difficulties he had to deal with. Every day he had to visit four different offices in his town. In addition, his predecessor left him the responsibility of several committees where he was expected to do all the work. Everything conspired to keep him from prayer.

Various difficulties make a full prayer life almost impossible. But thank God the things which are impossible with men are possible with God! God's call to prayer need not be a burden nor a cause of guilt. He means for it to be a joy. Through prayer He can give us strength for all we do and bring down His power to work through us in the lives of others.

Let us confess the sin that shames us and then confront it in the name of our Redeemer. The same light that shows us our sin and condemns us for it will show us the way out of it. Deficiency in our Christian life is the root cause of unfaithfulness in prayer. God will use this discovery to bring us both the power to pray that we long for and also the joy of a new and healthy life, of which prayer is the spontaneous expression.

Lord God, may I be attentive to the teaching of Your Spirit as I continue to learn about prayer. Amen.

HEALTH FOR THE SOUL

He was amazed to see that
no one intervened to help the oppressed.

ISAIAH 59:16

How can our lack of prayer be transformed into a blessing? How can it be changed into the path where evil may be conquered?

How can our relationship with the Father become one of continual prayer?

We must begin by going back to God's Word to study the place God intends for prayer to have in the life of His child. A fresh understanding of what prayer is and what our prayers can be will free us from our wrong attitudes concerning the absolute necessity of continual prayer.

We need insight into how reasonable this divine appointment is. We need to be convinced of how it fits in with God's love and our happiness. Then we will be freed from the false impression of prayer being an arbitrary demand. We will yield to it and rejoice in it as the only way for the blessing of heaven to come to earth. It will no longer be a task and burden of self-effort and strain. As simple as breathing is in the physical life, so will praying be in the Christian life that is led by the Spirit.

Our failure in the prayer life is a result of our failure in the Spirit life. Any thought of praying more and of praying effectively will be in vain unless we are brought into closer intimacy with our Lord. His life of prayer on earth and of intercession in heaven is breathed into us in the measure that our surrender and our faith allow.

Lord God, enable us for the work of intercession which is the greatest need of the Church and the world today. Amen.

MINISTRATION OF
THE SPIRIT AND PRAYER

If you sinful people know how to give good gifts to your children,
how much more will your heavenly Father give
the Holy Spirit to those who ask him.

LUKE 11:13

Jesus said: "Keep on asking, and you will be given what you ask for." God's giving is inseparably connected with our asking. He applied this principle especially to the Holy Spirit. As surely as a father gives bread to his child, so God gives the Holy Spirit to those who ask. The whole ministration of the Spirit is ruled by the one great law: God must give, we must ask. When the Holy Spirit was poured out at Pentecost, it was in answer to prayer.

Along with our confession of the lack of prayer, we also need an understanding of the place prayer occupies in God's plan of redemption. Nowhere is this clearer than in the first half of the Acts. The outpouring of the Holy Spirit at the birth of the Church is the true measure of the presence of the Spirit.

The Spirit came in answer to prayer. "They all met together continually for prayer. . . ." Then there follows, "On the day of Pentecost, seven weeks after Jesus' resurrection, the believers were meeting together in one place. . . . And everyone present was filled with the Holy Spirit. . . . Those who believed. . .were added to the church—about three thousand in all" (Acts 1:14; 2:1, 4; 2:41).

The Holy Spirit had been promised by Christ. He sat down on His throne and received the Spirit from the Father. But one more thing was needed: the ten days of united, continued supplication of the disciples.

Lord, make me aware that I need to pray in the power of the Spirit.
May we, Your Church, pray—believing that You will answer. Amen.

Spiritual Roots

After this prayer,
the building where they were meeting shook,
and they were all filled with the Holy Spirit.

Acts 4:31

Definite, determined prayer is what we need. Peter and John had been threatened with punishment. When they returned to their friends, they lifted up their voices to God with one accord. When they prayed, "the building where they were meeting shook, . . . they preached God's message with boldness."

It is as if the story of Pentecost is repeated (the prayer, the filling with the Spirit, the speaking God's Word with boldness), in order to imprint permanently on the Church that it is prayer that lies at the root of the spiritual life and power of the Church. The degree with which God gives His Spirit is determined by our asking.

Later people complained about the neglect of the Grecian Jews in the distribution of alms. The apostles proposed the appointment of deacons to serve the tables. "Then we can spend our time in prayer and preaching and teaching the word" (Acts 6:4). There is nothing in honest business that prevents fellowship with God. Least of all should ministering to the poor hinder the spiritual life. And yet the apostles felt it would hinder their ministry of prayer and the Word.

What does this teach? Maintenance of the spirit of prayer is possible in many kinds of work, but it is not enough for those who are the leaders of the Church. They need to communicate with the King and keep the heavenly world in clear focus for the maintenance of their own spiritual life and also for those around them.

Lord, continue my instruction each day. Keep me in proper spiritual
focus and empower me for the work to be done. In Jesus' name, amen.

A HIGHER GIFT

"Your prayers and gifts to the poor
have not gone unnoticed by God!"

ACTS 10:4

At Samaria Philip had preached with great blessing and many believed. But the Holy Spirit had not yet fallen on them. The apostles sent Peter and John to pray for them that they might receive the Holy Spirit.

The power for such prayer was a higher gift than preaching. It was the work of men who had been in closest contact with the Lord. Of all the gifts of the early Church, there is none more needed than the gift of prayer. This power is given to those who say, "We will give ourselves to prayer."

The outpouring of the Holy Spirit in the house of Cornelius provides another testimony to the interdependence of prayer and the Spirit. Peter went up to pray on the housetop. He saw heaven opened and there came a vision that revealed the cleansing of the Gentiles. Then came the message of the men from Cornelius, a man who "prayed regularly" and had heard from an angel, "Your prayers. . .have not gone unnoticed by God." Then the voice of the Spirit was heard saying, "Go with them" (Acts 10:20).

It is a praying Peter to whom the will of God is revealed and who is brought into contact with a praying and prepared company of hearers. In answer to all this prayer comes blessing beyond all expectation, and the Holy Spirit is poured out upon the Gentiles.

Father, by the power of Your Spirit may I reorder my priorities so that
faithful prayer has the right place in my life. I ask in Jesus' name,
amen.

STONE WALLS GIVE WAY

But while Peter was in prison,
the church prayed very earnestly for him.

ACTS 12:5

When we pray consistently we will receive an entrance into God's will of which we would otherwise know nothing. We will receive blessing above all we ask or think. The teaching and power of the Holy Spirit are unalterably linked to prayer.

The power that the Church's prayer has is shown not only as the apostles pray but also as the Christian community does. In Acts 12 Peter is in prison awaiting execution. The death of James had aroused the Church to a sense of great danger; the thought of losing Peter, too, wakened all their energies. They went to prayer.

Prayer was effective; Peter was delivered. When he came to the house of Mary he found "many were gathered for prayer" (Acts 12:12). Double chains, soldiers, and the iron gate—all gave way before the power from heaven that prayer brought to his rescue. The power of the Roman Empire was nothing in the presence of the power that the Church wielded in prayer.

Those Christians stood in close and living relationship with their Lord. They knew well that the words "I have been given complete authority" and "And be sure of this, I am with you always" were absolutely true. They had faith in His promise to hear them whatever they asked. They prayed in the assurance that the powers of heaven not only could work on earth but that they would work at the Church's request on its behalf.

Lord God of power, may we see Your power at work as Your prayerful
followers did in the early Church. Amen.

LINKING WITH THE KING

So after more fasting and prayer,
the men laid their hands on them
and sent them on their way.

ACTS 13:3

A cts names five men at Antioch who had dedicated themselves to ministering to the Lord with prayer and fasting.
The Holy Spirit met them and gave them insight into God's
plans. He called them to be fellow workers with Himself. There
was a work to which He called Barnabas and Saul. The five men's
part would be to send Barnabas and Saul with renewed fasting
and prayer and to let them go, sent forth by the Holy Spirit.

God in heaven would not send His chosen servants without
the cooperation of His Church. People on earth were to have a
partnership in the work of God. Prayer prepared them for this.
The Holy Spirit gave authority to praying Christians to do His
work and use His name. It was through prayer the Holy Spirit
was given. Prayer is still the only secret of true Church exten-
sion—prayer that is guided from heaven to find and send forth
God-called and God-empowered men and women.

In answer to prayer the Holy Spirit will indicate the people
He has selected. In response to prayer that sets them apart under
His guidance, He will give the honor of knowing that they are
people sent forth by the Holy Spirit. Prayer links the King on the
throne with the Church at His footstool. The Church, the human
link, receives its divine strength from the power of the Holy
Spirit, who comes in answer to prayer.

Lord, may I always pray with expectation, knowing that You will
grant my request because Your Holy Spirit lives in me. Amen.

A LIVING CONNECTION

Jesus Christ is the same yesterday, today, and forever.

HEBREWS 13:8

In the history of the Church two great truths stand out. Where there is much prayer, there will be much of the Spirit; where there is much of the Spirit, there will be ever-increasing prayer. When the Spirit is given in answer to prayer, it stimulates more prayer to prepare for a fuller revelation and communication of His divine power and grace. If prayer was the power by which the early Church flourished and triumphed, is it not the one need of the Church today?

Perhaps these should be considered axioms in our ministries:

1. Heaven is still as full of stores of spiritual blessing as it was then.
2. God still delights to give the Holy Spirit to those who ask Him.
3. Our life and work are still as dependent on the direct impartation of divine power as they were in Pentecostal times.
4. Prayer is still the appointed means for drawing down these heavenly blessings in power on ourselves and those around us.
5. God still seeks for men and women who will, with all their other work of ministering, specially give themselves to persevering prayer.

Lord God, make all these truths live in us. May we not rest until they have mastered us and our whole heart is so filled with them that we count the practice of intercession as our highest privilege. In Jesus' name, amen.

A MODEL OF INTERCESSION

They will pray to the LORD day and night
for the fulfillment of his promises.
Take no rest, all you who pray.

ISAIAH 62:6

Then, teaching them more about prayer, he [Jesus] used this illustration: 'Suppose you went to a friend's house at midnight, wanting to borrow three loaves of bread. You would say to him, "A friend of mine has just arrived for a visit, and I have nothing for him to eat." He would call out from his bedroom, "Don't bother me. The door is locked for the night, and we are all in bed. I can't help you this time." But I tell you this—though he won't do it as a friend, if you keep knocking long enough, he will get up and give you what you want so his reputation won't be damaged' " (Luke 11:5–8).

Prayer is the one power on earth that commands the power of heaven. The early days of the Church are a great object lesson of what prayer can do. Prayer can pull down the treasures of heaven into earth.

Prayer is both indispensable and irresistible. Unknown blessing is stored up for us in heaven; that power will make us a blessing to men and enable us to do any work or face any danger. It is the one secret of success. It can defy all the power of the world and prepare men to conquer that world for Christ.

In all this prayer there was little thought of personal need or happiness. Rather there was desire to witness for Christ and bring Him and His salvation to others. It was the thought of God's kingdom and glory that possessed these disciples. We, too, must enlarge our hearts for the work in intercession.

Thank You for the privilege of prayer, Father. Thank You for providing access to Your throne through Jesus. Amen.

THE URGENT NEED

*"If you keep knocking long enough,
he will get up and give you what you want
so his reputation won't be damaged."*

LUKE 11:8

By intercession our faith, love, and perseverance will be aroused. How may we become more successful in prayer? In the parable of the friend at midnight, Jesus teaches us that intercession for the needy calls forth our power of prevailing prayer. Intercession is the most perfect form of prayer; it is the prayer Christ ever lives to pray on His throne.

Intercession has its origin in urgent need. The friend came at midnight. He was hungry and could not buy bread. If we are to learn to pray as we should, we must open our eyes and hearts to the needs around us.

We hear of the billions of unreached people living in midnight darkness, perishing for lack of the bread of life. We hear of millions of nominal Christians, the majority almost as ignorant and indifferent as the heathen. We see millions in the Church, not indifferent, and yet knowing little of the power of a life fed by bread from heaven. If we believe what we profess, that God certainly will help in answer to prayer, this ought to make intercessors of us. It should motivate us to give our lives to prayer for those around us.

Let's face the need—Christless souls perishing of hunger, while there is bread enough and to spare! Our own neighbors and friends, people entrusted to us, die without hope! Christians around us live fruitless lives! Prayer is needed.

Lord, give Your Church—give me—a passion to pray for the souls of others. In Jesus' name, amen.

WILLING LOVE

" 'A friend of mine has just arrived for a visit,
and I have nothing for him to eat.' "

LUKE 11:6

The friend took his weary, hungry friend into his house and into his heart, too. He did not excuse himself by saying he had no bread. At midnight he went out to seek food for him. He sacrificed his night's rest and his comfort to find the needed bread. Love "does not demand its own way" (1 Corinthians 13:5). It is the very nature of love to forget itself for the sake of others. It takes their needs and makes them its own. It finds real joy in living and dying for others as Christ did.

The love of a mother for her prodigal son makes her pray for him. When we have true love for others we will have the spirit of intercession. It is possible to do much faithful and earnest work for others without true love for them. Just as a lawyer or a physician, out of a love of their profession and a high sense of faithfulness to duty, may become deeply involved with the needs of clients or patients without any special love for them, so servants of Christ may give themselves to their work with devotion and self-sacrificing enthusiasm without any strong, Christlike love. It is this lack of love that causes a lack of prayer. Love will compel us to prayer as that love and diligence are combined with the tender compassion of Christ.

Lord, I need Your tender compassion and the love that will compel me to prayer. May I not rest in my work if others are not saved. I ask in Jesus' name, amen.

THE SENSE OF INADEQUACY

" 'Don't bother me. The door is locked for the night,
and we are all in bed. I can't help you this time.' "

LUKE 11:7

W e often speak of the power of love. In one sense this is
true, and yet the truth has limitations. The strongest
love may be utterly inadequate. A mother might be willing to
give her life for her dying child but still not be able to save it.
The host at midnight was most willing to give his friend bread,
but he had none. It was this sense of inadequacy that sent him
begging, "A friend of mine has just arrived. . .and I have nothing for him to eat." This sense of inadequacy gives strength to
the life of intercession.

"I have nothing for him to eat." As we are aware of our
inadequacies, intercession becomes the only hope and refuge. I
may have knowledge, a loving heart, and be ready to give myself
for those under my charge, but I cannot give them the bread of
heaven. With all my love and zeal, still "I have nothing to set
before them."

Blessed are you if you have made "I have nothing" the
motto of your ministry. You think of the judgment day and the
danger of those without Christ and recognize a supernatural
power is needed to save people from sin. You feel utterly insufficient—all you can do is to meet their natural need. "I have
nothing" motivates you to pray. Intercession appears to you as
the only thing in which your love can take refuge.

Dear Jesus, may I remember that a sense of inadequacy is the heart of
intercession. I come to You in weakness, asking for Your blessing on all
those who are in need. Amen.

FAITH IN PRAYER

"Suppose you went to a friend's house at midnight
wanting to borrow three loaves of bread."

LUKE 11:5

What the man in Luke 11 has not, another can supply. He has a rich friend nearby who will be both able and willing to give the bread. He is sure that if he only asks, he will receive. This faith makes him leave his home at midnight. If he himself has not the bread to give, he can ask another.

We need this simple, confident faith that God will give. Where that faith really exists, there will surely be no possibility of our not praying. In God's Word we have everything that can motivate and strengthen such faith in us. The heaven our natural eye sees is one great ocean of sunshine, with its light and heat giving beauty and fruitfulness to earth. In the same manner, Scripture shows us God's true heaven, which is filled with all spiritual blessings—divine light and love and life, heavenly joy and peace and power—all shining down upon us. It reveals to us our God waiting, even delighting, to bestow these blessings in answer to prayer.

Many promises and testimonies in Scripture call and urge us to believe that prayer will be heard. What we cannot possibly do ourselves for those whom we want to help can be done and received by prayer. Surely there is no question as to our believing that prayer will be heard.

Lord, I know that through prayer the poorest and weakest can give blessings to the needy. May I, even though poor, be used to make many rich. In Jesus' name, amen.

PERSISTENCY THAT PREVAILS

" 'Don't bother me.
The door is locked for the night,
and we are all in bed.
I can't help you this time.' "

LUKE 11:7

The faith of the host in Luke 11 met a sudden and unexpected obstacle—the rich friend refuses to hear: "I can't help you this time." The loving heart had not counted on this disappointment and cannot accept it. The asker presses his threefold plea: Here is my needy friend; you have abundance, I am your friend. Then he refuses to accept a denial. The love that opened his house at midnight and then left it to seek help must conquer.

Here is the central lesson of the parable: In our intercession we may find that there is difficulty and delay in the answer. It may be as if God says, "I can't help you this time." It is not easy to hold fast our confidence that He will hear and then to continue to persevere in full assurance that we shall have what we ask. Even so, this is what God desires from us. He highly prizes our confidence in Him, which is essentially the highest honor the creature can render the Creator. He will therefore do anything to train us in the exercise of this trust in Him. Blessed the man who is not staggered by God's delay or silence or apparent refusal, but is strong in faith giving glory to God. Such faith perseveres, importunately if need be, and cannot fail to inherit the blessing.

Father, when You delay in answering my prayers I sometimes think the worst and wonder if You have determined not to listen to my request. Help me to be persistent and to never fail to trust You. In Jesus' name, amen.

CERTAINTY OF A RICH REWARD

"But I tell you this—though he won't do it as a friend,
if you keep knocking long enough, he will get up and
give you what you want so his reputation won't be damaged."

LUKE 11:8

O h that we might believe in the certainty of an abundant answer! Would that all who find it difficult to pray much would focus on the reward and in faith trust the divine assurance that their prayer cannot be in vain.

If we will only believe in God and His faithfulness, intercession will become the very first thing we do when we seek blessing for others. It will be the very last thing for which we cannot find time. It will become a thing of joy and hope because we recognize that we are sowing seed that will bring forth fruit a hundredfold. Disappointment is impossible: "But I tell you this—though he won't do it as a friend, if you keep knocking long enough, he will get up and give you what you want so his reputation won't be damaged" (Luke 11:8).

Time spent in prayer will yield more than time given to work. Only prayer gives work its worth and its success. Prayer opens the way for God Himself to do His work in and through us. Let our primary ministry as God's messengers be intercession; in it we secure the presence and power of God.

"Suppose you went to a friend's house at midnight, wanting to borrow three loaves of bread" (Luke 11:5). This friend is none other than our God. In the darkness of midnight, in the greatest need, when we have to say of those we care for "I have nothing for him to eat," let us remember that we have a rich Friend in heaven.

Father, Creator of the universe, thank You for Your generosity to Your followers. Thank You for the promise of answered prayer. May we trust without wavering. Amen.

Start Now

Commission Joshua and encourage him.

DEUTERONOMY 3:28

Let us confess before God our lack of prayer. Lack of prayer is the proof of the lack of faith. It is the symptom of a life that is not spiritual—that is still under the power of self and the flesh and the world. Let us by faith in the Lord Jesus give ourselves to be intercessors. May every sight of those needing help, every stirring of the spirit of compassion, every sense of our own inadequacy to bless, every difficulty in the way of our getting an answer, all combine to urge us to do this one thing: with perseverance cry to God who alone can and will help.

If we indeed feel that we have failed in a life of intercession until now, let us do our utmost to train a young generation of Christians to profit by our mistake and avoid it. Moses could not enter the land of Canaan, but there was one thing he could do. He could at God's bidding "commission Joshua and encourage him." If it is too late for us to make good our failure, let us at least encourage those who come after us to enter into the good land, the blessed life of unceasing prayer.

Father, may I as an intercessor give to others what I receive from You day by day. In Jesus' name, amen.

BECAUSE OF HIS PERSISTENCE

"If you keep knocking long enough,
he will get up and give you what you want
so his reputation won't be damaged."

LUKE 11:8

One day Jesus told His disciples a story to illustrate their need for constant prayer and to show them that they must never give up. . . . Then the Lord said, 'Learn a lesson from this evil judge. Even he rendered a just decision in the end, so don't you think God will surely give justice to his chosen people who plead with him day and night? Will he keep putting them off? I tell you, he will grant justice to them quickly!' " (Luke 18:1, 6–8).

Our Lord Jesus thought it so important for us to know the need of perseverance in prayer that He gave two parables to teach us. This aspect of prayer contains prayer's greatest difficulty and its highest power. In prayer we must expect difficulties which can be conquered only by determined perseverance.

In the first parable Jesus tells us that our Father is more willing to give good things to those who ask than any earthly father is to give his child bread. In the second He assures us that God longs to grant justice to His elect.

Urgent prayer is not needed because God must be made willing. The need lies in ourselves. He uses the unwilling friend and the unjust judge to teach that perseverance can overcome every obstacle.

The difficulty is in our incapacity to receive the blessing. Because of our lack of spiritual preparedness, there is a difficulty with God, too. His wisdom, His righteousness, even His love, dare not give us what would do us harm if we received it too soon or too easily.

Help me, Lord, to respond to difficulties in prayer by being persistent,
not by giving up. In Jesus' name, amen.

A Strengthening Prayer Life

*"Listen to me! You can pray for anything,
and if you believe, you will have it."*

MARK 11:24

The consequence of sin that makes it impossible for God to give at once is a barrier on God's side as well as ours. The attempt to break through the power of sin is what makes the striving and the conflict of prayer such a reality.

Throughout history people have prayed with a sense that there were difficulties in the heavenly world to overcome. They pleaded with God for the removal of the unknown obstacles. In that persevering supplication they were brought into a state of brokenness, of entire resignation to Him, and of faith. Then the hindrances in themselves and in heaven were both overcome. As God prevails over us, we prevail with God.

God has made us so that the more clearly we see the reasonableness of a demand, the more heartily we will surrender to it. One cause of our neglecting prayer is that there appears to be something arbitrary in the call to such continued prayer. This apparent difficulty is a divine necessity and is the source of unspeakable blessing.

Try to understand how the call to perseverance and the difficulty that it throws in our way is one of our greatest privileges. In the very difficulty and delay will the true blessedness of the heavenly life be found. There we learn how little we delight in fellowship with God and how little we have of living faith in Him. There we learn to trust Him fully and without reservation. There we truly come to know Him.

Though it is very difficult, Lord, I ask that You would continue to teach me through the delays and difficulties associated with prayer. In Jesus' name, amen.

DIFFICULT PRAYER

He prayed more fervently,
and he was in such agony of spirit that his sweat
fell to the ground like great drops of blood.

LUKE 22:44

Have you ever noticed how much difficulties play a part in our life? They call forth our power as nothing else can. They strengthen character.

All nature has been so arranged by God that nothing is found without work and effort. Education is developing and disciplining the mind by new difficulties which the student must overcome. The moment a lesson has become easy, the student is advanced to one that is more difficult. It is in confronting and mastering difficulties that our highest accomplishments are found.

It is the same in our relationship with God. Imagine what the result would be if the child of God had only to kneel down, ask, get, and go away. Loss to the spiritual life would result. Through difficulties we discover how little we have of God's Holy Spirit. There we learn our own weakness and yield to the Holy Spirit to pray in us. There we take our place in Christ Jesus and abide in Him as our only plea with the Father. There our own will and strength are crucified. There we rise in Christ to newness of life. Praise God for the need and the difficulty of persistent prayer as one of His choice means of grace.

Think what Jesus owed to the difficulties in His path. He persevered in prayer in Gethsemane, and the prince of this world with all his temptation was overcome.

Lord Jesus, in persevering prayer may I walk with You and learn of crucifixion. May I share in the fellowship of Your cross. Amen.

Persistence in Prayer

"You can pray for anything,
and if you believe, you will have it."

Mark 11:24

Persistence has various elements—the main ones are perseverance, determination, and intensity. It begins with the refusal to readily accept denial. This develops into a determination to persevere, to spare no time or trouble, until an answer comes. This grows in intensity until the whole being is given to God in supplication. Boldness comes to lay hold of God's strength. At one time it is quiet; at another, bold. At one point it waits in patience, but at another, it claims at once what it desires. In whatever different shape, persistence always means and knows that God hears prayer; I must be heard.

Think of Abraham as he pleads for Sodom. Time after time he renews his prayer until he has to say, "Please don't be angry, my Lord" (Genesis 18:30). He does not cease until he has learned how far he can go, has entered into God's mind, and has rested in God's will. For his sake Lot was saved. "God had listened to Abraham's request and kept Lot safe" (Genesis 19:29).

Think of Jacob when he feared to meet Esau. The angel of the Lord met him and wrestled with him. When the angel saw that he did not prevail, he said, "Let me go." Jacob said, "I will not let you go" (Genesis 32:26). So the angel blessed him there. That boldness pleased God so much that a new name was given to Jacob: Israel, he who strives with God, "because you have struggled with both God and men and have won" (Genesis 32:28).

Lord, I would become one who perseveres in prayer. I would learn to claim and take Your blessing. In Jesus' name, amen.

Pray and Prevail

The earnest prayer of a righteous person
has great power and wonderful results.

James 5:16

When Israel had made the golden calf, Moses returned to the Lord and said, "Alas, these people have committed a terrible sin. . . . But now, please forgive their sin—and if not, then blot me out of the record you are keeping" (Exodus 32:31–32). That was persistence. Moses would rather have died than not have his people forgiven.

When God had heard him and said He would send His angel with the people, Moses came again. He would not be content until, in answer to his prayer, God himself should go with them. God had said, "I will indeed do what you have asked" (Exodus 33:17). After that in answer to Moses' prayer, "Let me see your glorious presence" (Exodus 33:18), God made His goodness pass before him. Then Moses at once began pleading, "O Lord, then please go with us" (Exodus 34:9). "Moses was up on the mountain with the LORD forty days and forty nights" (Exodus 34:28).

Moses was persistent with God and prevailed. He proves that the person who truly lives near to God shares in the same power of intercession which there is in Jesus.

James teaches us to pray for each other. "The earnest prayer of a righteous person has great power and wonderful results." Praise God! He still waits for us to seek Him. Faith in a prayer-hearing God will make a prayer-loving Christian.

Thank You, Lord, for the examples in Scripture of men such as Moses. May I learn from them that prayer accomplishes much. In Jesus' name, amen.

THE MARK OF A PRAYING CHRISTIAN

The earnest prayer of a righteous person
has great power and wonderful results.

JAMES 5:16

Remember the marks of the true intercessor: a sense of the need of those without Christ, a Christlike love, an awareness of personal inadequacy, faith in the power of prayer, courage to persevere in spite of refusal, and the assurance of an abundant reward. These are the qualities that change a Christian into an intercessor.

These are the elements that mark the Christian life with beauty and health. They fit a person for being a blessing in the world. These are the attitudes that call forth the heroic virtues of the life of faith.

Nothing shows more nobility of character than the spirit of enterprise and daring which battles major difficulties and conquers. So should we who are Christians be able to face the difficulties that we meet in prayer. As we "work" and "strive" in prayer, the renewed will asserts its royal right to claim what it will in the name of Christ.

We should fight our way through to the place where we can find liberty for the captive and salvation for the perishing. The blessings which the world needs must be called down from heaven in persevering, believing prayer.

Our work is often insignificant due to our little prayer. Let us change our method and make unceasing prayer be the proof that we look to God for everything and that we believe that He hears us.

Holy Spirit, answer our prayer. Take complete possession of us to do Your work through us. Amen.

THE LIFE THAT CAN PRAY

I chose you.
I appointed you to go and produce fruit that will last,
so that the Father will give you whatever you ask for,
using my name.

JOHN 15:16

O ur power in prayer depends upon our life. When our life is right, we will know how to pray in a way pleasing to God, and our prayer will be answered. "If you stay joined to me," our Lord says, "you may ask any request you like, and it will be granted!" (John 15:7). According to James it is the prayer of a righteous man that "has great power and wonderful results" (James 5:16).

In the parable of the vine Jesus taught that the healthy, vigorous Christian may ask what he or she wishes and will receive it. He says, "If you stay joined to me and my words remain in you, you may ask any request you like, and it will be granted." Again He says, "You didn't choose me. I chose you. I appointed you to go and produce fruit that will last, so that the Father will give you whatever you ask for, using my name" (John 15:16).

What life must one lead to bear fruit? What must a person be in order to pray with results? What must one do to receive what he or she asks? The answer is simple. Live as a branch depending on the vine for strength. The source of power in prayer is the vine. If we are branches, abiding in Christ, the vine, He will supply the power. If we trust the vine, then we can ask what we wish and it will be granted.

Lord Jesus, may we live more and more as branches of You, the Vine.
May much fruit result from our prayers. Amen.

BEARING FRUIT

The earnest prayer of a righteous person
has great power and wonderful results.

JAMES 5:16

A branch is a growth of the vine, produced to bear fruit. It has only one purpose: that through it the vine may bear and ripen its fruit. As the vine lives to produce the sap that makes the grape, so the branch receives that sap and bears the grape. Its work is to serve the vine so that, through the branch, the vine may do its work.

The believer, the branch of Christ the heavenly Vine, is to live exclusively so Christ may bear fruit through him. A true Christian is to be devoted to the work of bearing fruit to the glory of God.

With our life abiding in Him, and His words abiding and ruling in our hearts, there will be grace to pray as we should and faith to receive whatever we ask.

The promises of our Lord's farewell discourse appear to us too large to be taken literally. We rationalize them to meet our human ideas of what we think they ought to be. We separate them from the life of devotion to Christ's service for which they were given.

God's covenant is: give all and take all. One who is willing to be nothing but a branch of Christ, the Vine, will receive liberty to claim Christ's riches in all their fullness and the wisdom and humility to use them properly.

Lord Jesus, thank You for Your wonderful promises to those who abide in You. May I live life as Your branch so that I may experience Your leading and blessing. Amen.

ASK AND IT WILL BE DONE

Dear friends, if our conscience is clear,
we can come to God with bold confidence.

1 JOHN 3:21

Think for a moment of the men of prayer in Scripture and see in them lives that could pray in power. Abraham was an intercessor. What gave him such boldness? He knew that God had called him away from his home and people to walk with Him so that all nations might be blessed in him. He knew that he had obeyed and forsaken all for God. Implicit obedience, to the very sacrifice of his son, was the law of his life. He did what God asked, so he dared to trust God to do what he asked.

Moses was an intercessor. He, too, had forsaken all for God and lived at God's disposal. Often it is written of him that he did what the Lord commanded. No wonder he was very bold. His heart was right with God. He knew God would hear him.

We only pray the way we live. God longs to prove himself the faithful God and mighty helper of His people. He waits to answer praying hearts wholly turned from the world and to Himself.

The branch that abides in Christ, the heavenly Vine, will bear fruit in the salvation of others. Such people may dare ask what they will—and it shall be done.

Father, help me in my weakness to abide in You so that I ask and it shall be done. My every hope and confidence is in You. I pray in Jesus' name, amen.

PRUNING FOR PRAYER

He prunes the branches that do bear fruit
so they will produce even more.

JOHN 15:2

The more aware we become of our inability to pray in power, the more we are helped to press on toward the secret of power in prayer. Jesus said, "I am the true vine, and my Father is the gardener" (John 15:1). We not only have Jesus Himself. We have the Father, as the husbandman, watching over our growth and fruit-bearing. It is not left to our faith. God Himself will see to it that the branch is what it should be. He will enable us to bring forth just the fruit we were appointed to bear. "He prunes the branches that do bear fruit so they will produce even more." The Father seeks more fruit. More fruit is what the Father Himself will provide.

Of all fruit-bearing plants there is none that produces so much wild wood as the vine. Every year it must be pruned. It is like this for the Christian. The branch that desires to abide in Christ and bring forth fruit must yield itself to divine cleansing.

The gardener cuts away true, honest wood that the branch has produced. It must be pruned because it draws away the strength of the vine and hinders the flow of the juice to the grape. The luxuriant growth of wood must be cast away so that abundant life may be seen in the cluster.

There are things in you that sap your interest and strength. They must be pruned. Pruning results in a life that can pray.

I am grateful, Lord, that You are a loving gardener. I trust myself into Your loving care and ask You to prune me that I may bear much fruit. Amen.

Is Prayerlessness Sin?

I will not remain with you any longer
unless you destroy the things among you
that were set apart for destruction.

JOSHUA 7:12

I f we are to deal effectively with the lack of prayer, we must ask, "Is it sin?" Jesus is Savior from sin. When we experience sin, we can know the power that saves from sin. The life that can pray effectively is one that knows deliverance from the power of sin. But is prayerlessness sin?

Experiencing the presence of God is the great privilege of God's people and their power against the enemy. Throughout Scripture the central promise is that God is with us. The whole-hearted person lives consciously in God's presence.

Defeat and failure are due to the loss of God's presence. This was true at Ai. God brought His people into Canaan with the promise of victory. With the defeat at Ai, Joshua knew that the cause must be the withdrawal of God's power. God had not fought for them.

In the Christian life defeat is a sign of the loss of God's presence. If we apply this to our failure in prayer, we see that it is because we are not in full fellowship with God.

The loss of God's presence is due to sin. Just as pain is nature's warning of a physical problem, defeat is God's voice telling us there is something wrong. He has given Himself wholly to His people. He delights in being with them. He never withdraws himself unless they compel Him to do so by sin.

I am grateful, Lord, for Your presence. May I not lose it through the sin of prayerlessness. Where I fail, forgive me and restore me to close fellowship. In Jesus' name, amen.

REVEALED SIN

"As for me, I will certainly not sin against the LORD
by ending my prayers for you.
And I will continue to teach you what is good and right."

1 SAMUEL 12:23

We may think we know what sin is keeping us from prayer, but only God can truly reveal it. For example, after the defeat at Ai, He spoke to Joshua. "Israel has sinned and broken my covenant." Israel had sinned. God Himself revealed it.

God must reveal to us that the lack of prayer is a greater sin than we have thought. It means we have little taste for fellowship with God. Our faith rests more on our own work than on the power of God. We are not ready to sacrifice ease for time with God.

When the pressure of work becomes the excuse for not finding time in His presence, there is no sense of absolute dependence upon God. There is no full surrender to Christ.

If we would yield to God's Spirit, all our excuses would fall away and we would admit that we had sinned. Samuel once said, "As for me, I will certainly not sin against the LORD by ending my prayers for you. And I will continue to teach you what is good and right" (1 Samuel 12:23). Ceasing from prayer is sin against God.

When God discloses sin it must be confessed and cast out. If we have reason to think prayerlessness is the sin that is in "our camp," let us begin with personal and united confession. With God's help let us put away and destroy the sin. Then we can know His presence and power.

Father, help me listen in prayer as You disclose my sin. Then I will confess it and, with Your help, cast the sin out of my camp so I can know Your presence and power. Amen.

GOD'S PRESENCE RESTORED

Restore to me again the joy of your salvation.

PSALM 51:12

When sin is cast out, God's presence is restored. This truth is so simple. God's presence restored means victory secured. Then, if there is defeat, we are responsible for it. Sin somewhere is causing it. We need to discover the sin and repent. The moment the sin is put away, we may confidently expect God's presence.

God never speaks to His people of sin except with the purpose of saving them from it. The same light that shows the sin will show the way out of it. The same power that condemns will give the power to rise up and conquer.

God is speaking to us about this sin: "He was amazed to see that no one intervened to help the oppressed" (Isaiah 59:16). The God who says this will work the change in His children when they seek His face. He will make the shame of sin confessed a door of hope. Let us simply confess that we have sinned; we dare not sin any longer.

In the matter of prayer God does not demand impossibilities. He does not give us an impracticable ideal. He does not ask us to pray without giving the grace to enable us to do so. Believe Him. He will give the grace to do what He asks.

Father, I bow in stillness and wait before You. Overshadow me with Your presence. Deliver me from the sin of prayerlessness. I trust You to forgive me and to teach me to pray. Amen.

THE SECRET OF EFFECTIVE PRAYER

"You can pray for anything,
and if you believe,
you will have it."

MARK 11:24

The more we enter into the mind of our Lord and think about prayer as He thinks, the more His words will grow in us. They will produce in us their fruit—a life corresponding to the truth they contain. Christ, the living Word of God, gives in His words a power which brings into existence what they say. This power accomplishes in us what He asks. It equips us for what He demands. View His teaching on prayer as a promise of what He, by His Holy Spirit, is going to build into your character.

The Lord gives us the five essential elements of prayer:

— the heart's desire
— the expression of that desire in prayer
— the faith that carries the prayer to God
— the acceptance of God's answer
— the experience of the desired blessing

Each Christian can say, "I want to ask and receive in faith the power to pray just in the way and just as much as my God expects of me." During the next few days let us meditate on our Lord's words in the confidence that He will teach us how to pray for this blessing.

I look forward, Lord, to learning how to pray as You want me to. Give me the understanding and grace to do so. In Jesus' name, amen.

DESIRE

"You can pray for anything,
and if you believe,
you will have it."

MARK 11:24

D esire is the power that moves our whole world and directs the course of each person. Desire is the soul of prayer. The cause of insufficient prayer is often the lack of desire. Some may doubt this. They are sure they have earnestly desired what they ask. But if they judge whether their desire has been as whole-hearted as God would have it, they may see that it was the lack of desire that caused the failure.

What is true of God is true of each of His blessings. "If you look for me in earnest, you will find me when you seek me" (Jeremiah 29:13).

We may have a strong desire for spiritual blessings. But alongside them are other desires occupying a large place in our interests. The spiritual desires are not all-absorbing. We are puzzled that our prayer is not heard. It is because God wants the whole heart. If there are desires which occupy more of our heart than He Himself, the desires that we are praying for cannot be granted.

We desire the gift of intercession, grace and power to pray as we should. Our hearts must give up other desires; we must give ourselves wholly to this one. By focusing on the blessedness of this grace, by believing with certainty that God will give it to us, desire may be strengthened. The first step will have been taken toward the possession of the desired blessing.

Father, help me to pray with deep longings. May I please You by bringing petitions that I desire with my whole heart. Amen.

EXPRESS YOUR DESIRES

"You can pray for anything,
and if you believe,
you will have it."

MARK 11:24

The desire of the heart must become the expression of the lips. The Lord Jesus more than once asked those who cried out to Him what they wanted. He wanted them to say what they desired. To declare it brought them into contact with Him and wakened their expectation. To pray is to enter into God's presence, to have distinct dealing with Him, to commit our need to Him and to leave it there. In so doing we become fully conscious of what we are seeking.

There are some who often carry strong desires in their heart but don't bring them to God in a clear expression of repeated prayer. There are others who go to the Word and its promises to strengthen their faith but do not pointedly ask God to fulfill them. Therefore their heart does not gain the assurance that the matter has been put into God's hands. Still others come in prayer with so many requests and desires that it is difficult for them to say what they really expect God to do.

If you want God to give you this gift of faithfulness in prayer and power to pray as you should, begin to pray about it. Declare to yourself and to God.

Here is something I have asked and am continuing to ask 'til I receive. My Father! I do ask and expect of You the grace of prayer and intercession. Amen.

FAITH

*"You can pray for anything,
and if you believe,
you will have it."*

It is only by faith that we receive Jesus Christ or live the Christian life. Faith also is the power of prayer. If we are to have our prayer for the grace of prayer answered, we must begin to pray in faith as never before.

Faith is the opposite of sight. They are contrary to each other. "We live by believing and not by seeing" (2 Corinthians 5:7). If heart and prayer are to be full of faith, we must withdraw from the visible. The person that seeks to enjoy life, who gives first place to the duties of daily life, is inconsistent with a strong faith.

"We don't look at the troubles we can see right now." The negative action needs to be emphasized if the positive—"rather, we look forward to what we have not yet seen" (2 Corinthians 4:18)—is to become natural to us. In praying, faith depends upon our living in the invisible world.

The reason for our lack of faith is our lack of knowledge of God and communion with Him. Jesus said to have faith in God when He spoke of removing mountains. When a soul knows God, and allows the light of God to illuminate his life, unbelief will become impossible. All the mysteries connected with answers to prayer—however little we may be able to solve them intellectually—will be swallowed up in the assurance that this God is our God. He does answer prayer. He will delight to give the grace to pray that I am asking for.

Lord, I believe in You and trust You. Give me the grace to pray with power and persistence. Amen.

Accept the Answer

*"You can pray for anything,
and if you believe,
you will have it."*

MARK 11:24

Faith must accept the answer given by God in heaven before it is found on earth. This is the essence of believing prayer. Spiritual things can only be spiritually grasped. The spiritual blessing of God's answer to your prayer must be accepted in your spirit before you see it physically. Faith does this.

A person who not only seeks an answer, but first seeks after the God who gives the answer, receives the power to know that he has obtained what he has asked. If he knows that he has asked according to God's will, he believes that he has received.

There is nothing so heart-searching as this faith, "if you believe, you will have it." As we strive to believe, and find we cannot, we are compelled to discover what hinders us. Blessed are those who, with their eyes on God alone, refuse to rest 'til they have believed what our Lord bids. Here is the place where faith prevails, and prevailing prayer is born out of human weakness. Here enters the real need for persevering prayer that will not rest or go away or give up 'til it knows it is heard and believes that it has received.

Lord Jesus, give me the Spirit of supplication. Change any focus in my life that is on self and not on You. Enable me to overcome the pressures of daily life which hinder prayer. Give me my heart's desire—grace to pray much and in Your spirit, as You would have me do. In Your name, amen.

EXPERIENCE THE BLESSING

"You can pray for anything,
and if you believe,
you will have it."

MARK 11:24

Receiving from God in faith the answer with perfect assurance that it has been given is not necessarily the possession of the gift we have asked for. At times there may be a long interval before we have it physically. In other cases we may enjoy at once what we have received. When the interval is long we have need of faith and patience. We need faith to rejoice in the assurance of the answer bestowed and to begin to act upon that answer though for the present there is no visible proof of its presence.

We can apply this principle to our prayer for the power to be faithful intercessors. Hold fast to the divine assurance that as surely as we believe, we receive. Rejoice in the certainty of an answered prayer. The more we praise God for it, the sooner will the experience come. We may begin at once to pray for others in the confidence that grace will be given us to pray with more perseverance and more faith than we have done before.

If we do not find an immediate increase in our desire to pray, this must not discourage us. We have accepted a spiritual gift by faith; in that faith we are to pray, doubting nothing. We may count upon the Holy Spirit to pray in us, even though it is with groanings which cannot find expression. In due time we shall become conscious of His presence and power.

Holy Spirit, give me faith to persevere in prayer. Whether the practice of prayer is difficult or not, may I know Your presence in my prayer life. In Jesus' name, amen.

THE SPIRIT'S PRESENCE

"And be sure of this:
I am with you always,
even to the end of the age."

MATTHEW 28:20

When the Lord chose His twelve disciples, it was "to be his regular companions" and that He might "send them out to preach" (Mark 3:14). A life in fellowship with Him was to be their preparation for fulfilling the Great Commission.

When Christ spoke of His leaving them to go to the Father, their hearts were filled with great sorrow. The presence of Christ had become indispensable to them; they could not think of living without Him. To comfort them, Christ gave them the promise of the Holy Spirit, which would be a heavenly presence far more intimate than they had ever known.

Unbroken fellowship with Him was the power the disciples would need to preach and to testify of Him. When Christ gave them the Great Commission to go into all the world and preach the gospel to every creature, He added the words: "And be sure of this: I am with you always, even to the end of the age."

This principle forever holds true for all His servants. Without the experience of His presence always abiding with us, our daily walk will have no power. The secret of our strength is in the Spirit of Jesus Christ being with us every moment, inspiring and directing and strengthening us. As you pray, be deeply convinced of Christ's words: "And be sure of this: I am with you always."

Heavenly Father, I thank You for the gift of Your indwelling Holy Spirit. Breathe into my heart, with divine power, Your comforting words: "I am with You always!" In Jesus' name, amen.

THE OMNIPOTENCE OF CHRIST

"I have been given complete authority
in heaven and on earth."

MATTHEW 28:18

Before Christ gave His disciples their Great Commission, He first revealed Himself in His resurrected power as a partner with God Himself. It was the faith of this that enabled the disciples to undertake their mission with boldness.

Just think of what the disciples had learned of the power of Christ Jesus when He was here on earth. Yet that was little compared with the greater works that He would do in and through them. Christ provided the power to work even in the feeblest of His servants with the strength of the almighty God.

We, too, are to count literally upon the daily experience of being "strong with the Lord's mighty power" (Ephesians 6:10). But remember, this power is never meant to be experienced as if it were our own. It is only as Jesus Christ as a living person dwells and works within our own heart and life that there can be power in our prayer and personal testimony. It was when Christ had said to Paul, "My power works best in your weakness," that he could say what he had never learned to say before: "When am I weak, then am I strong" (2 Corinthians 12:9–10). It is the disciple of Christ who truly understands that all power has been entrusted to Christ and that we must receive that power from Him hour by hour.

Dear Father, I acknowledge my weakness. By the power of Your risen Son, may Your strength be made perfect in my weakness. In the power of Jesus' name, amen.

THE OMNIPRESENCE OF CHRIST

"I will be with you."

EXODUS 3:12

When Christ said to His disciples, "I have been given complete authority in heaven and on earth," the promise immediately followed, "I am with you always" (Matthew 28:18, 20). The Omnipotent One is truly the Omnipresent One. The writer of Psalm 139 speaks of God's omnipresence as something beyond his comprehension: "Such knowledge is too wonderful for me, too great for me to know!" (verse 6).

The revelation of God's omnipresence in the man Christ Jesus makes the mystery still deeper. The fact that we can experience this presence every moment is inexpressibly wonderful. And yet many of us find it difficult to understand all that Christ's presence implies and how, through prayer, it can become the practical experience of our daily life.

When Christ says "always," He means to give us the assurance that there should never be a moment in which that presence cannot be our experience. Yet, it does not depend upon what we can effect, but upon what He undertakes to do.

The omnipotent Christ is indeed the omnipresent Christ. His promise to us is: "I am with you always." Let your faith in Christ, the Omnipresent One, be in the quiet confidence that He will be with you every day and every moment. Meet Him in prayer, and let His presence be your strength for service.

Father, I marvel that You would want to be with me every moment of my life. Such a thought "is too wonderful for me." May I earnestly seek and know Your presence daily. In Jesus' name, amen.

CHRIST THE SAVIOR OF THE WORLD

"He is indeed the Savior of the world."

JOHN 4:42

Omnipotence and omnipresence are what are called natural attributes of God. They have their true worth only when linked to and inspired by His moral attributes, holiness, and love. What lies at the root of these attributes is His divine glory as the Savior of the world and Redeemer of all men. It was because He humbled Himself and became obedient unto death that God so highly exalted Him. His share in the attributes of God was owing to the work He had done in His perfect obedience to the will of God. His finished redemption made salvation possible for humanity.

It is only when His servants demonstrate that they obey Him in all His commands that they can expect the fullness of His power and His presence to be with them. It is only when they are living witnesses to Christ's redemptive power to save and to keep from sin that they can experience His abiding presence. Then they will have the power to train others to the life of obedience that He asks.

The abiding presence of our Savior is promised to all who have accepted Him in the fullness of His redeeming power. What a privilege to meet in prayer with the One who has redeemed us. Our lives and words should proclaim to the world what a wonderful Savior He is.

Heavenly Father, through the power of Your Son, You have chosen to save and indwell me. May I be a living witness of Your goodness and power to those around me. In Your saving name, amen.

CHRIST CRUCIFIED

God forbid that I should boast about anything
except the cross of our Lord Jesus Christ.

GALATIANS 6:14

Christ's highest glory is His cross. It was in this that He glorified the Father and the Father glorified Him. In the fifth chapter of Revelation, Christ receives the worship of the ransomed and the angels and all creation. And it is as the Crucified One that His servants have learned to say: "God forbid that I should boast about anything except the cross of our Lord Jesus Christ." Is it not reasonable that Christ's highest glory should be our only glory, too?

It is the crucified Jesus who promises, "I am with you always" (Matthew 28:20). One reason why we may find it so difficult to expect and enjoy His abiding presence is because we do not glory in the cross. We have been crucified with Christ; our "old sinful selves were crucified with Christ" (Romans 6:6). This means we are crucified to the world and are free from its power. Consequently, we are to deny ourselves—to have the mind that was in Christ. He emptied Himself and took the form of a servant. He humbled Himself and became obedient even to the death of the Cross.

As we pray, it is the crucified Christ who comes to walk with us and in whose power we are to live the life that can say: "Christ crucified lives in me."

Heavenly Father, what a mystery it is to glory in the cross of Christ. May I always have the mind of Christ and, in so doing, be crucified to the world. In Jesus' name, amen.

CHRIST GLORIFIED

*For the Lamb who stands in front of the throne
will be their Shepherd.*

REVELATION 7:17

A nd be sure of this: I am with you always" (Matthew 28:20).
Who is it that speaks these words? We must take time to
know Him well if we are to understand what we can expect
from Him as He offers to be with us every day. Who is He?
None other than the Lamb who had been slain in the midst of
the throne! The Lamb in His deepest humiliation is enthroned
in the glory of God. This is He who invites me to the closest
fellowship with Himself.

It takes time in adoring worship and prayer to come under
the full impression that Christ, before whom all heaven bows,
is the One who offers to be my companion. He desires to lead
me like a shepherd and to make me one of those who follows
Him wherever He goes.

Read Revelation 5 until your heart is possessed by the
thought that all heaven falls prostrate before Christ, and the
elders cast their crowns before the throne. The Lamb reigns
amid the praises and the love of His ransomed ones and the
praises of all creation. And if this is He who comes to me in my
daily life and offers to walk with me, I cannot expect Him to
abide with me unless my heart bows in surrender to a life of
prayer, praise, and service.

*Dear Father, Your Son, Jesus, is the embodiment of the omnipotent
glory of the everlasting God and of His love. I am awed that You
would passionately desire to fellowship with me day by day. In Your
glorious name, amen.*

THE GREAT QUESTION

Jesus asked them,
"Do you believe I can make you see?"
"Yes, Lord," they told him, "we do."

MATTHEW 9:28

Jesus told her. . .'Those who believe in me, even though they die like everyone else, will live again. . . . Do you believe this?' 'Yes, Lord,' " she told Him. From what we have seen and heard of Christ Jesus, our hearts are ready to say with Martha: "I have always believed you are the Messiah, the Son of God, the one who has come into the world from God" (John 11:25–27). But when it comes to believing Christ's promise to us of His abiding presence, we do not find it so easy to say, "I believe." Yet it is this faith that Christ desires to work within us.

We must understand clearly what the conditions are on which Christ offers to reveal to us the secret of His abiding presence. God will not force His blessings on us against our will. He seeks in every possible way to stir our desire and to help us to realize that He is able and willing to make His promises true. The resurrection of Christ from the dead is His great, all-prevailing evidence.

Now the great question is whether we are willing to take Him at His word and rest in the promise: "I am with you always." Christ's question to us is: "Do you believe?" Let us not rest until we have bowed before Him in prayer and said: "Yes, Lord, I do believe."

Dear God, Your promise to be with me is forever true. With a grateful heart I respond to You: Yes, Lord, I do believe. In the name of Your Son, Jesus, amen.

CHRIST REVEALING HIMSELF

"Those who obey my commandments are the ones who love me. And because they love me, my Father will love them, and I will love them."

JOHN 14:21

C hrist had promised the disciples that the Holy Spirit would come to reveal His presence with them. When the Spirit came, Christ showed Himself to them in a new, spiritual way. They would know Him far more intimately than they ever had while He was on earth.

The condition of this revelation of Himself is based on one word—love: "Those who obey my commandments are the ones who love me. And because they love me, my Father will love them, and I will love them." This is the meeting of Divine and human love. The love with which Christ had loved them had taken possession of their hearts, and they would demonstrate that love by full and absolute obedience. The Father would see this, and Christ would respond to their loving hearts by revealing Himself to them.

But Christ doesn't just promise to reveal Himself to us. He also promises to dwell in the heart that loves Him. "My Father will love them, and we will come to them and live with them" (John 14:23). It is within the heart that is fully surrendered, showing itself in love and obedience, that the Father and the Son will take up residence.

Christ's promise remains the same today: "And be sure of this: I am with you always." Oh, that everyone would believe and prayerfully claim the blessed promise: "I will reveal myself to each one of them."

Dear Father, You have chosen to reveal Yourself to the heart that loves You. I surrender my heart in obedience and love so that I may experience Your blessed presence. In Jesus' name, amen.

MARY: THE MORNING WATCH

"Mary!" Jesus said.
She turned toward him and exclaimed, "Teacher!"

JOHN 20:16

Here we have the first manifestation of the risen Savior—to Mary Magdalene, the woman who loved Jesus so much.

Think of what the morning watch meant to Mary. Is it not a proof of the intense longing of a love that would not rest until it had found the Lord? It meant a separation from all else in her longing to find Christ. It meant the struggle of fear against a faith that refused to let go its hold of Christ's wonderful promise: "Those who obey my commandments are the ones who love me. . .and I will love them. And I will reveal myself to each one of them" (John 14:21).

That first morning watch, waiting in prayer for the risen Lord to reveal Himself, has been a joy to thousands of souls! With a burning love and strong hope, they wait for Jesus to manifest Himself as the Lord of Glory. There they learn to dwell in the keeping of His abiding presence.

There is nothing that can prove a greater attraction to our Lord than the love that sacrifices everything and rests satisfied with nothing less than Himself. It is to such a love that Christ reveals Himself. He loved us and gave Himself for us. It is to our love that He speaks the word: "And be sure of this: I am with you always" (Matthew 28:20). It is love that accepts, rejoices, and lives in that word.

Dear Lord, this morning I wait expectantly for You to reveal Yourself to me. Breathe upon me the power of Your Resurrection life and presence. In the name of Jesus, amen.

EMMAUS: THE EVENING PRAYER

As they sat down to eat. . . .
Suddenly, their eyes were opened,
and they recognized him.

LUKE 24:30–31

M ary teaches us what the morning watch can mean for the revelation of Jesus to the soul. Emmaus reminds us of the place that the evening prayer has in preparing for the full manifestation of Christ in the soul.

When Jesus Himself approached the two disciples as they traveled, they did not recognize Him. But as the Lord spoke with them, their hearts began to burn within them. Yet they never thought that it might be Christ Himself. How often does Jesus come near with the purpose of manifesting Himself to us, and yet we don't see Him?

When Jesus told the two disciples He must continue on His journey, their plea to spend the night caused Him to stay. We, too, should reserve time toward the end of the day when our whole heart prays with the urgency that constrains Him.

So what was it that led our Lord to reveal Himself to these two men? Nothing less than this: their intense devotion to their Lord. There may be much ignorance and unbelief, but if there is a burning desire that longs for Christ, He will make Himself known to us. In such intense devotion and constraining prayer, the Lord will open our eyes and we will know Him and enjoy the secret of His abiding presence.

Dear Lord, at the close of this day please stay awhile longer and abide with me. Open my eyes to see the full manifestation of Yourself. In Jesus' name, amen.

THE DISCIPLES: THEIR DIVINE MISSION

Suddenly, Jesus was standing there among them!
"Peace be with you," he said.

JOHN 20:19

The disciples had received Mary's message of Christ's resurrection. Late in the evening the men from Emmaus told how He had been made known to them. Now their hearts were prepared for when Jesus stood in their midst and said, "Peace be unto you," and showed them His hands and His feet. "They were filled with joy when they saw their Lord! He spoke to them again and said, 'Peace be with you. As the Father has sent me, so I send you'" (John 20:20–21).

With Mary, He revealed Himself to her fervent love that could not rest without Him. With the men at Emmaus, it was their constraining prayer that received the revelation. Here He meets the willing servants whom He had trained for His service. He changes their fear into boldness to carry out the work the Father had entrusted to them.

For this divine work they needed nothing less than divine power. He breathed upon them the resurrection life and fulfilled the promise He gave: "For I will live again, and you will, too" (John 14:19).

The word is spoken to us, too: "As the Father has sent me, so I send you. . . . Receive the Holy Spirit" (John 20:21–22). If our hearts are set on nothing less than the presence of the living Lord, we can be confident that it will be given to us. Jesus never sends His servants out without the promise of His abiding presence and His almighty power.

Heavenly Father, with a heart of love and constraining prayer, I ask for Your presence. May Your presence and power be mine for Your service today. Amen.

THOMAS:
THE BLESSEDNESS OF BELIEVING

"Blessed are those who haven't seen me and believe anyway."

JOHN 20:29

C hrist revealed Himself and allowed Thomas to touch His hands and His side. No wonder Thomas could find no words but those of holy adoration: "My Lord and my God." And yet Christ said: "You believe because you have seen me. Blessed are those who haven't seen me and believe anyway."

True, living faith gives a far deeper and more intimate sense of Christ's divine nearness than even the joy that filled the heart of Thomas. Thomas had proved his intense devotion to Christ when he said, "Let's go, too—and die with Jesus" (John 11:16). To such a love, even when it was struggling with unbelief, Jesus Christ revealed Himself.

We, too, can experience the presence and power of Christ in a far deeper reality than Thomas did. To those who have not seen Jesus and yet believe, He has promised that He will reveal Himself and that the Father and He will come and dwell in them.

Yet we are often inclined to think of this full life of faith as something beyond our reach. Such a thought robs us of the power to believe. Take prayerful hold of Christ's word: "Blessed are those who haven't seen me and believe anyway." This blessing only comes by the faith that receives the love and the presence of the living Lord.

Jesus, You are the one object of my desire and confidence. I have not seen You, yet I believe in Your Word, Your divine power, and Your abiding presence. In Your trustworthy name, amen.

PETER: THE GREATNESS OF LOVE

He said, "Lord, you know everything.
You know I love you." Jesus said, "Then feed my sheep."

JOHN 21:17

In Christ's appearances after His death, it was to the intense devotion of the prepared heart that He revealed Himself. Now in the manifestation of Himself to Peter, it is again love that is the keynote.

We can easily understand why Christ asked the question three times, "Do you love me?" It was to remind Peter of the terrible self-confidence in which he had said: "No! Not even if I have to die with you! I will never deny you!" (Matthew 26:35). Peter was clearly in need of prayerful soul-searching so he could be sure that his love was true. He needed to understand that true love was the one thing needed for the full restoration to his place in the heart of Jesus.

God is love. Christ is the Son of His love. "I have loved you even as the Father has loved me" (John 15:9). Jesus asked that His disciples prove their love to Him by keeping His commandments and loving each other.

To everyone who longs to have Jesus reveal Himself, the essential requirement is love. Peter teaches us that such love it is not in the power of man to offer. If the self-confident Peter could be changed so dramatically, we must believe that Christ will work that change in us, too. He will then reveal Himself to that loving heart in all the fullness of His precious word: "And be sure of this: I am with you always" (Matthew 28:20).

Dear Father, remove every hint of self-confidence and pride that hinders our relationship. Please give me a divine love that will find its place in Your heart. In Jesus' name, amen.

John: Life from the Dead

*"Don't be afraid! I am the First and the Last.
I am the living one who died. Look,
I am alive forever and ever!"*

Revelation 1:17–18

Sixty or more years after the resurrection, Christ revealed Himself to the beloved disciple. John immediately fell as dead at His feet. We learn from this that man's sinful nature cannot see the vision of the divine glory and live. It needs the death of the natural life in order for the life of God to enter in.

Christ then laid His hand on John and said, "Don't be afraid! . . .I am the living one who died. Look, I am alive forever and ever!" He reminded John that He, too, had passed through death so He could rise to the life and the glory of God. For the Master Himself and for every disciple, there is only one way to the glory of God—death to sin and self.

This lesson is a necessary one. Fellowship with Jesus—and the experience of His living power—is not possible without the sacrifice of all that there is in us of the world and its sin. The disciples experienced this reality when Christ made this great charge to them: deny self, bear the cross, and follow Me.

Let us accept this lesson—through death to life. Since Christ's death now works in us, we must yield ourselves in prayer to His power and let Him live in and through us.

Heavenly Father, You have asked me to lose my life for Your sake. As I die to the world, sin, and self, let me experience the full life of Your abiding presence. In the name of the risen Lord, amen.

PAUL: CHRIST REVEALED IN HIM

For it pleased God in his kindness
to choose me and call me. . . .
Then he revealed his Son to me.

GALATIANS 1:15–16

Paul tells us that it pleased God to reveal His Son in him. He gives his testimony to the result of that revelation: "Christ lives in me" (Galatians 2:20). The chief mark of that life is that he is crucified with Christ. This enables him to say, "I no longer live." In Christ Paul had found the death of self. Just as the cross is the chief characteristic of Christ, so the life of Christ in Paul made him inseparably one with his crucified Lord. So completely was this the case that he could say: "God forbid that I should boast about anything except the cross of our Lord Jesus Christ. Because of that cross, my interest in this world died long ago" (Galatians 6:14).

So if Christ actually lived in Paul so that he no longer lived, what became of his responsibility? His answer was clear: "I live my life in this earthly body by trusting in the Son of God, who loved me and gave himself for me" (Galatians 2:20). Paul's life was a life of faith in Christ, who had loved him and had given Himself completely for him. Consequently, Christ had undertaken at all times to be the life of His willing disciple.

The indwelling Christ was the secret of his life of faith, his power in prayer, the one aim of all his life and work. Let us believe in the abiding presence of Christ as the sure gift to each one who trusts Him fully.

Heavenly Father, I ask for Your abiding presence today. May I be so dead to myself and the world that people will only see You living in me. In Jesus' name, amen.

WHY COULD WE NOT?

*"But this kind of demon won't leave unless
you have prayed and fasted."*

MATTHEW 17:21

T he disciples had often cast out demons. But here they had been powerless. They asked the Lord what the reason might be. His answer is very simple: "You didn't have enough faith."

How is it that we cannot live that life of unbroken fellowship with Christ which the Scripture promises? Simply because of our unbelief. We do not realize that faith must accept and expect that God will, by His almighty power, fulfill every promise He has made. We do not live in that utter helplessness and dependence on God alone which is the very essence of faith. We are not strong in the faith, fully persuaded that what God has promised He is able and willing to perform.

But what is the reason why this faith is so often lacking? "But this kind of demon won't leave unless you have prayed and fasted." To have a strong faith in God requires a life in close touch with Him by persistent prayer. We cannot call up faith at our bidding; it needs close communion with God through prayer. It needs the denial of self—the sacrifice of a worldly heart. Just as we need God to give us faith and power, He, too, needs our whole being to be utterly given up to Him. Prayer and fasting are essential to this.

Dear Father, I often do not live in utter dependence upon You. Thus I find myself powerless to live the life of faith. Help me to deny all else and rest only in Your strength. Amen.

THE POWER OF OBEDIENCE

"And the one who sent me is with me—
he has not deserted me.
For I always do those things that are pleasing to him."

JOHN 8:29

In these words Christ tells us what His life with the Father was. At the same time, He reveals the law of all communion with God—simple obedience.

In John 14 He says three times: "If you love me, obey my commandments" (verses 15, 21, 23); also in chapter 15: "When you obey me, you remain in my love, just as I obey my Father and remain in his love. . . . You are my friends if you obey me" (verses 10, 14).

Obedience is the proof and the exercise of the love of God in our hearts. It comes from love and leads to love. It assures us that we are abiding in the love of Christ. It seals our claim to be called the friends of Christ. So it is not only a proof of love but of faith, too. It assures us that we "will receive whatever we request because we obey him and do the things that please him" (1 John 3:22).

Obedience enables us to abide in His love and gives us the full experience of His unbroken presence. It is to the obedient that the word comes—"And be sure of this: I am with you always" (Matthew 28:20—and to whom all the fullness of its meaning will be revealed.

Father, You have said: "I will write [my laws] on their hearts" (Jeremiah 31:33). "I will put my Spirit in you so you will obey my laws and do whatever I command" (Ezekiel 36:27). May my full obedience to Your Word bring the joy of Your abiding presence. In Your Son's name, amen.

THE POWER OF INTERCESSION

Then we can spend our time in prayer
and preaching and teaching the word.

ACTS 6:4

I n his travels throughout Asia, Dr. Mott was moved by the need for united prayer in the missionary endeavor. He writes: "There is no better way to serve the deepest interest of the Church than by multiplying the number of real intercessors and by focusing their prayers on those situations which demand the almighty working of the Spirit of God. Far more important than any service we can give to missions is that of helping to release the superhuman energy of prayer. Immeasurably more important than any other work is the linking of all we do to the fountain of divine life and energy. The Christian world not only has a right to expect mission leaders to set forth the facts and methods of the work, but also a larger discovery of superhuman resources and spiritual power."

And where is there a greater need of focusing the united intercession of Christians than on the great army of missionaries? They tell of their need for the presence and the power of God's Spirit in their life and work. They long for the experience of the abiding presence and power of Christ every day. They need it; they have a right to it. Shouldn't we become a part of that great army that pleads with God for the power which is so absolutely necessary for effective work?

Dear Father, it is clear that the effectiveness of Your work relies on the releasing of Your power through prayer. May we continue steadfastly in prayer until Your power is sent forth. Amen.

The Power of Time

My times are in thy hand.

PSALM 31:15 KJV

My time is in Your hand. It belongs to You. You alone have a right to command it. I yield it wholly and gladly to Your disposal." What mighty power time can exert if wholly given up to God!

Time is lord of all things. The history of the world is proof of how, slowly but surely, time has made man what he is today. All around us we see the proofs, such as the growth of a child to manhood. It is under the law of time and its inconceivable power that we spend our lives.

This is especially true in communion with God—all on the one condition: that we have sufficient time with God. Yet we often confess the weakness of our spiritual life and the inadequate results of our work. This is due to the failure to take time for daily communion with God.

What can be the cause of this sad confession? Nothing less than a lack of faith in the God-given assurance that time spent alone with Him will indeed bring into our lives the power to do His work.

Through prayer, submit your timetable to the inspection of Christ and His Holy Spirit. A new life will be yours if you fully believe and put into daily practice the words: "My time is in Your hand."

Dear God, I confess how often I allow my schedule to be filled with the unimportant, and I don't give enough time to You. Today I yield it wholly and gladly to Your disposal. In Jesus' name, amen.

The Power of Faith

"Anything is possible if a person believes."

MARK 9:23

Scripture teaches us that there is not one truth on which Christ insisted more frequently than the absolute necessity of faith and its unlimited possibilities. Experience has taught us that there is nothing in which we fall so short as the simple and absolute trust in God to literally fulfill in us all He has promised. A life in Christ's abiding presence must of necessity be a life of unceasing faith.

What are the marks of true faith? First of all, faith counts upon God to do all He has promised. It seeks nothing less than to claim every promise that God has made, in its largest and fullest meaning. It trusts the power of an almighty God to work wonders in the heart in which He dwells and rests in the hope of what He will do.

In the pursuit of the power which such a life of faith can give, our soul must take God at His word and claim the fulfillment of His promises. We must then look to Him, even in utter darkness, to perform what He has spoken.

The life of faith to which the abiding presence will be granted must have complete mastery of our whole being. This faith will be able to claim and experience the words of the Master: "And be sure of this: I am with you always" (Matthew 28:20).

Father, so often I am content to believe only some of Your promises. Through a faith which only You can inspire, I trust You to fulfill Your every promise. In Jesus' name, amen.

JOHN'S MISSIONARY

We are telling you about what we ourselves
have actually seen and heard,
so that you may have fellowship with us.

1 JOHN 1:3

This is the calling of the preacher of the gospel. His message is nothing less than to proclaim that Christ has opened the way for us simple men to have living fellowship with the holy God. He is to preach this as a witness to the life that he himself experiences. In the power of that testimony, he is to prove its reality and show how sinful man on earth can indeed live in fellowship with the Father and the Son.

The message suggests to us that the very first duty of the minister is to maintain close communion with God. He must be conscious of the fact that his life and conversation are the proof that his preaching is true, so that his words will appeal with power to the heart.

It is this living testimony that will encourage and compel us to surrender ourselves to Christ. It is this intimate fellowship with Christ that is the secret of daily service and prayer. It has the power to inspire wholehearted devotion to His service. It is in this intimate and abiding fellowship with Christ that the promise "I am with you always" (Matthew 28:20) finds its meaning.

This is what all Christians need—an abiding fellowship with God that will divinely influence the workers and the converts with whom they come in contact.

Heavenly Father, I came to faith in Christ through one who faithfully proclaimed and lived the gospel. May my life also compel others to desire Your abiding presence. In the name of Your Son, Jesus, amen.

PAUL'S MISSIONARY MESSAGE

For this is the secret: Christ lives in you,
and this is your assurance that you will share in his glory.

COLOSSIANS 1:27

In Paul's mind, the very substance of his gospel was the indwelling Christ. He spoke of the "riches of the glory of this mystery—Christ in you, the assurance of glory." Though he had preached this gospel for so many years as a missionary, he still asked for prayer that he might make that secret known.

The complaint is often made in regard to our churches that, after a time, there appears to be no further growth and very little of the joy and power for bearing witness to Christ Jesus. The question comes whether the church at home is living in the experience of this indwelling Christ, so that the sons and daughters whom she sends out also know the secret. The answer is in Paul's missionary message which culminates in the words: "Christ in you. . .your assurance that you will share in his glory."

Paul deeply felt the need for prayer to enable him to give this message faithfully. Is there not a call to all those who pray for our missionaries, and to our missionaries themselves, to obtain the power that leads Christians into the enjoyment of their rightful heritage? May the church at home also share in the blessing of this truth.

Dear God, Your Word makes it clear how the prayer of Your people empowers those who deliver the Good News. May the result be that many will understand the meaning of the words: "Christ in You, the assurance of glory." Amen.

THE MISSIONARY'S LIFE

You yourselves are our witnesses—and so is God—
that we were pure and honest and faultless
toward all of you believers.

1 THESSALONIANS 2:10

Paul more than once appeals to what his converts had seen of his own life. So he says: "We can say with confidence and a clear conscience that we have been honest and sincere in all our dealings. We have depended on God's grace, not on our own earthly wisdom. That is how we have acted toward everyone, and especially toward you" (2 Corinthians 1:12). Christ had taught His disciples as much by His life as by His teaching. Paul also sought to be a living witness to the truth of all that he had preached about Christ.

Paul appeals to the example of his own life throughout his writings. In Philippians 4:9 Paul writes: "Keep putting into practice all you learned from me and heard from me and saw me doing, and the God of peace will be with you." In 1 Timothy 1:14, 16: "Oh, how kind and gracious the Lord was! He filled me completely with faith and the love of Christ Jesus. . . . Then others will realize that they, too, can believe in him and receive eternal life."

Let us believe that when Paul said, "I myself no longer live, but Christ lives in me" (Galatians 2:20), he spoke of an actual abiding of Christ in him. Christ was working in him to do all that was well-pleasing to the Father. While in prayer, do not rest until you can say, "The Christ of Paul is my Christ. His empowerment is mine too."

Father, too often my actions hide the Christ whom I should be revealing. Help me to manifest the character of Christ so others can see and understand His message. In Jesus' name, amen.

THE HOLY SPIRIT

He [the Holy Spirit] will bring me glory
by revealing to you whatever he receives from me.

JOHN 16:14

When our Lord spoke the words to the disciples in Matthew 28:20, "And be sure of this: I am with you always," they did not at first understand or experience their full meaning. At Pentecost they were filled with the Holy Spirit. It was then that the Spirit brought down into their hearts the new life of Christ's abiding presence.

All our attempts to claim to live that life of continuous communion with Christ will be in vain unless we yield ourselves completely to the power and indwelling of the Holy Spirit. For the Spirit of God to show us what He can enable us to be, He demands complete possession of our whole being.

Christ meant the promise of His abiding presence to be accepted as absolute, divine truth. "And God has given us his Spirit as proof that we live in him and he in us" (1 John 4:13). But this truth can only be experienced when the Spirit of God is known and believed in and obeyed.

We need to understand that the Holy Spirit came as God to make known the Son in us. He claims absolute subjection and is willing to take possession of our whole being and will enable us to fulfill all that Christ asks of us.

Heavenly Father, Your Word says: "Because they love me, my Father will love them, and I will love them. And I will reveal myself to each one of them" (John 14:21). I trust You to fulfill Your promise that "We will come to them and live with them" (verse 23). In Jesus' name, amen.

FILLED WITH THE SPIRIT

Let the Holy Spirit fill and control you.
Then you will sing psalms and hymns and spiritual songs
among yourselves, making music to the Lord in your hearts.

EPHESIANS 5:18–19

If we had the expression "filled with the Spirit" only in regard to the story of Pentecost, we might naturally think that it was something special and not meant for ordinary life. But our text teaches us that it is meant for every Christian and for everyday life.

To realize this more fully, think of what the Holy Spirit was in Christ Jesus and under what conditions He was, as man, filled with the Spirit. He received the Spirit when He was praying and yielded Himself as a sacrifice to God by going down into the sinner's baptism. Full of the Holy Spirit, He was led to the forty days' fasting, sacrificing the needs of the body to be free for fellowship with the Father and for victory over Satan. He even refused, when He was famished, to listen to the temptation of Satan to use His power to make bread to supply His hunger. And so He was led by the Spirit all through life until He, by the Spirit, offered Himself without blemish unto God.

In Christ, the Spirit meant prayer, obedience, and sacrifice. It is only as we are led by the Spirit that we can abide in Christ Jesus, conquer the flesh and the world, and live the life with God in prayer and service.

Dear Father, may my faith in Christ be the measure of my fullness of the Spirit. Help me to regard the fullness of the Spirit as indispensable for Your service. In the name of Jesus, amen.

THE CHRIST LIFE

Christ lives in me.

GALATIANS 2:20

Christ's life was more than His teaching, more than His work, even more than His death. It was His life in the sight of God and man that gave value to what He said and did and suffered. It is this life that He gives to His people and enables them to live it out before men.

It was the life in the new brotherhood of the Holy Spirit that made both Jews and Greeks feel that there was some superhuman power about Christ's disciples. They gave living proof of the truth that God's love had come down and taken possession of them.

Everything depends upon the life with God in Christ being right. It is the simplicity and intensity of our life in Christ Jesus, and of His life in us, that sustains us in our daily walk. It makes us conquerors over self and everything that could hinder the Christ life. Through prayer, it gives us the victory over the powers of evil.

The life in Christ must be everything to us because Christ Himself lives in us. When Jesus spoke the words "And be sure of this: I am with you always" (Matthew 28:20), He meant nothing less than this: "All day and every day, I am with you. I am the secret of your life, your joy, and your strength."

Dear God, I cannot live life apart from the life of Christ in me. Help me to understand that it is the experience of the life hid with Christ in God that enables me to meet and overcome every difficulty. In Jesus' name, amen.

The Christlike Life

Your attitude should be the same that Christ Jesus had.

PHILIPPIANS 2:5

W hat was the attitude that was in Christ Jesus? "Though he was God, he did not demand and cling to his rights as God. He made himself nothing; he took the humble position of a slave and appeared in human form. And in human form he obediently humbled himself even further by dying a criminal's death on a cross" (Philippians 2:6–8). Self-emptying and self-sacrifice, obedience to God's will, and love to men, even unto the death of the Cross—this was the character of Christ for which God so highly exalted Him. It is the character of Christ that we are to imitate. He was made in the likeness of men, so we could be conformed into the likeness of God.

Self-effacement and self-sacrifice that God's will might be done and that man might be saved—this was the attitude of Christ. He lived only to please God and to bless men.

Don't say that this is an impossibility. What is impossible with men is possible with God. We are called to work out this salvation of a Christlike character with fear and trembling; for "God is working in you, giving you the desire to obey him and the power to do what pleases him" (Philippians 2:13). As we pray, let this be our one aim: to have the attitude that was in Christ Jesus.

Dear Father, to effectively proclaim the gospel, I must first embody it in a character that is fully conformed to the likeness of Christ. On my own, this is impossible. But what is impossible with men is possible with God. In the name of Jesus, amen.

CHRIST, THE NEARNESS OF GOD

Draw close to God,
and God will draw close to you.

JAMES 4:8

It has been said that the holiness of God is the union of God's infinite distance from sinful man with God's infinite nearness in His redeeming grace. Faith must always seek to realize both the distance and the nearness.

In Christ, God has come very near to man. Now the command comes: If you want God to come still nearer, you must draw near to Him. The promised nearness of Christ Jesus expressed in the promise, "And be sure of this: I am with you always" (Matthew 28:20), can only be experienced as we draw near to Him.

This means that at the beginning of each new day, we must yield ourselves to His holy presence. It means a voluntary, intentional, and wholehearted turning away from the world to wait on God to make Himself known to our souls. It means making time to allow Him to reveal Himself. It is impossible to expect the abiding presence of Christ with us through the day without the daily exercise of strong desire and childlike trust in His word.

As you pray, let these words come to you with new meaning each morning: "Draw close to God, and God will draw close to you." Wait patiently and He will speak in divine power: "I am with you always."

Dear God, in the words of the hymn writer, "Prone to wander, Lord, I feel it; prone to leave the God I love." With Your power, cause my heart to draw near to Your heart, so I might daily enjoy the nearness of Your abiding presence. In the name of Jesus, amen.

LOVE

*Jesus knew that his hour had come
to leave this world and return to his Father.
He now showed the disciples the full extent of his love.*

JOHN 13:1

These are the opening words of the talk that Jesus had with His disciples in the last hours before He went to Gethsemane (John 13–17). They are the revelation of that divine love which was manifested in His death on the cross.

He begins with the new commandment: "to love each other in the same way that I love you" (John 15:12). The new life in Christ Jesus is to be the unfolding of God's love in Christ. He continues: "I have loved you even as the Father has loved me. Remain in my love. When you obey me, you remain in my love, just as I obey my Father and remain in his love. I command you to love each other in the same way that I love you. And here is how to measure it—the greatest love is shown when people lay down their lives for their friends" (John 15:9–13).

Can words make it plainer that the love with which the Father loved the Son is to be in us? If by prayer we are to claim His daily presence, it can only be as a relationship of infinite tender love between Him and us. This love must be rooted in the faith of God's love to Christ coming into our hearts and showing itself in obedience to His commandments and in love to one another.

Heavenly Father, it is only in the atmosphere of a holy, living love that the abiding presence of the loving Christ can be known. May the depth of the divine love expressed in Christ's promise "I am with you always" be realized in me today. Amen.

The Trial and Triumph of Faith

"Anything is possible if a person believes."

Mark 9:23

What a glorious promise: "Anything is possible if a person believes." Yet it is the greatness of this promise that constitutes the trial of faith. At first we do not really believe its truth. But when we have grasped it, then comes the real trial in the thought: Such a faith is utterly beyond my reach. But what constitutes the trial of faith soon becomes its triumph.

When the father of the child heard Christ say, "Anything is possible if a person believes," he felt that this would only cast him into deeper despair. How could his faith be able to work the miracle? Yet we read that the father believed that Jesus not only had the power to heal his child but also the power to inspire him with the needed faith. The impression Christ generated upon him produced the second miracle: that he could have such great faith. And with tears he cried, "I do believe, but help me not to doubt!" The very greatness of faith's trial was the greatness of faith's triumph.

Through our trials we can experience the abiding presence of Him who speaks to us now: "I am with you always." Let us wait upon God in prayer until we can say in faith, "I do believe."

Dear Father, I am entirely dependent on the power of Christ to enable me to claim all Your promises. May my faith triumph as I declare: "I can do everything with the help of Christ who gives me the strength I need" (Philippians 4:13). In the name of Jesus, amen.

Exceeding Abundantly

By his mighty power at work within us,
he is able to accomplish infinitely
more than we would ever dare to ask or hope.

EPHESIANS 3:20

I n the great prayer which Paul had just written, he had apparently reached the highest expression possible of the life to which God's mighty power could bring the believer. But Paul is not content. In this doxology he rises still higher and lifts us up to give glory to God as "able to accomplish infinitely more than we would ever dare to ask or hope." Pause for a moment to consider what "infinitely more" means.

Think of the words "he has given us all of his rich and wonderful promises" (2 Peter 1:4). Think of "the incredible greatness of his power for us who believe him. This is the same mighty power that raised Christ from the dead" (Ephesians 1:19–20). With these words Paul hopes to lift our hearts to believe that God is able to do "infinitely more than we would ever dare to ask or hope." The power of God that works in us is nothing less than the exceeding power that raised Christ from the dead. This should cause us to think that there is something that God will do in us that is beyond all our imagination.

As we worship Him in prayer, let us believe that the Almighty God, who is working in our hearts, is able and willing to fulfill every one of His exceeding great and precious promises.

Gracious Father, You find joy in fulfilling every one of Your exceeding great promises. Through Christ You proved that where sin abounded, Your grace abounded more exceedingly. I pray this with thanksgiving, amen.

THE DISPENSATION OF THE SPIRIT

"How much more will your heavenly Father
give the Holy Spirit to those who ask him."

LUKE 11:13

As he was meditating on prayer, the writer of a little book on prayer says: "I felt deeply that in this time of the working of the Holy Spirit, all we do in God's service is of little value unless it is inspired by the power of the Holy Spirit." This reminded me of the well-known text, "How much more will your heavenly Father give the Holy Spirit to those who ask him."

A priority for each of us every day should be asking the Father for the gift of the Holy Spirit to meet our daily needs. Without this we cannot please God nor can we be of any real help to others. Our prayer that our lives fulfill God's purpose must have its origin in God Himself, the highest source of power. Water cannot rise higher than its source. If the Holy Spirit prays through us as human channels, our prayers will rise again to God, who is their source. The prayers will be answered by God working in us. The Christian life of each one of us depends chiefly on the quality of our prayers and not on the quantity.

What material for deep meditation, for earnest prayer!

Heavenly Father, give me the Holy Spirit afresh for this day. Grant me now the working of Your Holy Spirit that I may learn to pray. In Jesus' name, amen.

THE FRUIT OF THE SPIRIT

But when the Holy Spirit controls our lives,
he will produce this kind of fruit in us: love, joy, peace. . . .

GALATIANS 5:22

T he first two lessons on prayer are: We must ask the Father
to give us the Spirit anew every morning, and then ask the
Spirit to teach us and help us. Here is a third lesson—commit
to memory today's text.

Christians often think that they only need to ask God to
teach them to pray and that He will do it at once. This is not
always the case. What the Spirit does is strengthen our spiritual
lives so we are able to pray better. When we ask Him to teach
us, it is important that we first of all surrender ourselves to the
working of the Spirit. This surrender consists in naming before
Him the fruit of the Spirit, with the earnest prayer to be filled
with this fruit.

Think of the first three—love, joy, peace—the three chief
characteristics of a strong faith life. Love: to God, to believers,
and to all men. Joy: the proof of the provision for every need of
courage and faith for all the work we have to do. Peace: the
blessed state of undisturbed rest and security in which God can
keep our hearts and minds.

In His last talk with the disciples, Christ used these words:
"Remain in his love. . .so that you will be filled with my joy"
(John 15:10–11). "I am leaving you with a gift—peace of mind
and heart" (John 14:27).

Holy Spirit, please make Your fruit reach perfection in me. Then may
I be able to pray as I should, always asking more and more of the heav-
enly Father, knowing He will answer. In Jesus' name, amen.

LED BY THE SPIRIT

For all who are led by the Spirit of God are children of God.

ROMANS 8:14

L et us think about four other fruits of the Spirit: patience, kindness, goodness, gentleness. These all denote attributes of God. They will reach maturity in us as we pray for the working of the Holy Spirit.

Patience—In the Old Testament God's patience was praised. All Scripture bears witness to the patience God had for sinful man. "No, he is being patient for your sake. He does not want anyone to perish, so he is giving more time for everyone to repent" (2 Peter 3:9). This attribute of the Spirit will enable us to exercise divine patience with all sin and wrong so that sinners may be saved.

Kindness—We read wonderful things in the Psalms about God's kindness. "For his unfailing love toward those who fear him is as great as the height of the heavens above the earth" (Psalm 103:11). God can enable us to show this same mercy toward those around us.

Goodness—"Only God is truly good" (Luke 18:19). All goodness comes from God, and He gives to His children as each heart asks and desires. This goodness is manifested in sympathy and love to all in need.

Gentleness—It was chiefly in God's Son that the divine gentleness was shown. Jesus says: "Let me teach you, because I am humble and gentle" (Matthew 11:29). The Holy Spirit longs to impart gentleness to our hearts.

These four attributes of God may be brought to maturity in our hearts by the Holy Spirit so that we may be like Jesus.

Lord Jesus, through Your Spirit, teach me to be patient, kind, good, and gentle so that people may be attracted to You. In Your name, amen.

THE SPIRIT OF FAITHFULNESS

We have the same kind of faith the psalmist had when he said,
"I believed in God, and so I speak."

2 CORINTHIANS 4:13

Have you memorized Galatians 5:22–23 yet? If not, it is important to do so. It will strengthen your desire to have the fruit of the Spirit in you. Your expectation of God's blessing will be increased. Let us consider the last two fruits of the Spirit—faithfulness and self-control.

When the disciples asked the Lord: "Why couldn't we cast out that demon?" His reply was: "This kind of demon won't leave unless you have prayed and fasted" (Matthew 17:19, 21). They lacked faithfulness. Even if they had prayed, they had not the enthusiasm and self-sacrifice needed for prevailing prayer. Here we see faith and self-control working together.

Faithfulness is a fruit of the Spirit. Such faithfulness believes God's Word, clings to Him, and waits in perfect trust that His power will accomplish all that He has promised.

Self-control enables us to use restraint, carefulness, and unselfishness in our desires and in all our relationships. Our goal should be: "We are instructed to turn from godless living and sinful pleasures. We should live in this evil world with self-control, right conduct, and devotion to God" (Titus 2:12). We should show self-control in all our dealings with the world and its temptations, seek to be righteous in doing God's will, and live in close communion with God Himself.

Memorize this text. Let the Holy Spirit lead you each day to the Father so that the fruit of the Spirit will be seen in all your actions.

Father, I long for my life to be characterized by the fruit of the Holy Spirit. Grant me this desire, for I ask in the name of Your Son, Jesus, amen.

WORSHIP GOD IN THE SPIRIT

We put no confidence in human effort.
Instead, we boast about what Christ Jesus has done for us.

PHILIPPIANS 3:3

Today let us worship God in the Spirit. We have come to the Father asking for the Holy Spirit. We have requested the guidance of the Holy Spirit. Now we begin to pray.

First we pray to God the Father, thanking Him for His blessings. We acknowledge our entire dependence on Him and express our trust in His love and care for us. We wait before Him until we have the assurance of His presence.

Then we direct our prayer to the Lord Jesus and ask for grace to abide in Him always, for without Him we can do nothing. We look to Him as our Lord, our preserver, our life, and give ourselves into His keeping.

Finally, we pray to the Holy Spirit. Ask Him to strengthen us so that what we have asked of the Father and the Son may happen. He is the dispenser of the power and gifts of the Father and of the Lord Jesus.

"We who worship God in the Spirit are the only ones who are truly circumcised. We put no confidence in human effort. Instead, we boast about what Christ Jesus has done for us." We have no power in ourselves to do good. We count on the Lord Jesus through the Holy Spirit to work in us. Take time to meditate on these things, asking God to grant His fruit in your life.

Heavenly Father, Lord Jesus, Holy Spirit, teach me to pray with faith so that my life will demonstrate Your power and Your gifts. Amen.

INTERCESSION

Pray for each other.

JAMES 5:16

There is value in intercession. It is an indispensable part of prayer. It strengthens our love and faith in what God can do, and it brings blessing and salvation to others. Prayer should be mainly for others, not for ourselves alone. Begin by praying for those near and dear to us, those with whom we live, that we may be of help to them and not a hindrance.

Pray for your friends and all with whom you come into contact. Pray for all Christians, especially for ministers and those in responsible positions.

Pray for those who do not yet know the Lord as their Savior. Make a list of the names of those God has laid upon your heart and pray for their conversion. Christ needs you to bring to Him in prayer the souls of those around you. Pray, too, for all poor and neglected ones. Pray for mission work. Use a mission calendar with daily subjects of prayer.

Do you think this will take too much time? Just think what an inconceivable blessing it is to help others through your prayers. Look to the Holy Spirit for further guidance. If morning is not the best time for you, schedule another time later in the day. Cultivate the attitude: "I am saved to serve."

Lord God, allow me to taste the great joy of knowing that I am living even as Jesus Christ lived on earth—to make Your love known to others. Give me the persistence and discipline to pray as I should. In Your name, amen.

TIME

"Couldn't you stay awake and watch with me even one hour?"

MATTHEW 26:40

E very minute spent in prayer is valuable. If ten minutes is all
the time you can give, see what you can do in that time.
Most people can spare more time. If you will only persevere
from day to day, time will come of its own accord.

Is it possible that Christians can say that they cannot afford
to spend a quarter or half an hour alone with God and His
Word? When a friend comes to see us, or we have to attend an
important meeting, or there is anything to our advantage or
pleasure, we find time easily enough.

But God has a right to us and longs for us to spend time
with Him, and we find no time for fellowship with Him. Even
God's own servants are so occupied with their own work that
they find little time for that which is all-important—waiting on
God to receive power from on high.

Dear child of God, let us never say, "I have no time for
God." Let the Holy Spirit teach us that the most important and
profitable time of the whole day is the time we spend alone
with God. Communion with God through His Word and
prayer is as indispensable to us as the food we eat and the air we
breathe. Whatever else is left undone, God has the first and
foremost right to our time.

*Lord God, forgive me when my attitude toward prayer is casual. In
the name of Your Son, Jesus, I ask for a heart that is ever growing in
its desire to spend time with You. Amen.*

THE WORD OF GOD

For the word of God is full of living power.

HEBREWS 4:12

I find it a great help to use God's Word in my prayers. If the Holy Spirit impresses a certain text upon my mind, I plead the promise. This habit increases our faith, reminds us of God's promises, and brings us into harmony with God's will. We learn to pray according to God's will and understand that we can only expect an answer when our prayers are in accordance with that will (1 John 5:14).

Prayer is like fire. Fire can burn brightly only if it is supplied with good fuel. That fuel is God's Word, which must be studied carefully and prayerfully. His Word must be taken into the heart and lived out in the life.

We are all familiar with the characteristics of a seed—a small grain in which the life-power of a whole tree slumbers. If it is placed in the soil, it will grow and increase and become a large tree.

Each word or promise of God is a seed containing a divine life in it. If I carry it in my heart by faith, love it, and meditate on it, it will slowly, surely spring up and bring forth the fruit of righteousness.

The Holy Spirit uses both the Word and prayer. Prayer is the expression of our human need and desire. The Holy Spirit teaches us to use the Word as a guide to what God will do for us.

Dear Lord, thank You for Your Word and for the role it has in my prayer life. Help me to apply in prayer what I learn from it. In Jesus' name, amen.

THE NAME OF CHRIST

And whatever you do or say,
let it be as a representative of the Lord Jesus,
all the while giving thanks through him to God the Father.

COLOSSIANS 3:17

At the close of your prayer time, it is always well to add a request for the Holy Spirit to "remind you of everything I myself [Jesus] have told you. . . ." (John 14:26) all through the day. Then the prayers of the morning will not be counteracted by the work of the day.

Read today's text once more, prayerfully. Have you ever realized that it is a command? Is it the aim of your life to obey it? This may be difficult, but it is not impossible or God would not have asked it of us. God's Word has a wonderful power to preserve the spirit of thanksgiving in our lives. When we get up in the morning, let us thank God for the rest of the night in the name of the Lord Jesus. In His name at night, thank Him for the mercies of the day. The ordinary daily life full of most ordinary duties will be lightened by the thought of what God has done for us for Christ's sake. Each ordinary deed will lead to thankfulness that He has given us the power to perform it.

At first it may seem impossible to remember the Lord Jesus in everything, yet the mere endeavor will strengthen us. The love of Christ will enable us to live all day in His presence.

Lord Jesus, may all my words and deeds be in Your name. May I have the full, childlike confidence that what I ask in Your name, I will receive. In Your name, amen.

THE SPIRIT GLORIFIES CHRIST

He will bring me glory by revealing to you
whatever he receives from me.

JOHN 16:14

To understand and experience the work of the Holy Spirit you must try to grasp the relationship of the Holy Spirit to the Lord Jesus. Our Lord said that the Spirit would come as a Comforter to the disciples. The Spirit would reveal Him in their hearts. The disciples held on to that promise—they would not miss their Lord but have Him with them always. This made them pray earnestly for the Holy Spirit, for they longed to have Jesus with them always.

This is the meaning of our text— "He will bring me glory by revealing to you whatever he receives from me." Where there is an earnest desire for the glory of Jesus in the heart of the believer, the Holy Spirit will preserve the presence of Jesus in our hearts.

We must not weary ourselves with striving after God's presence. We must quietly endeavor to abide in fellowship with Christ, to love Him and keep His commandments, and to do everything in the name of Jesus. Then we will be able to count upon the secret but powerful working of the Spirit within us.

If our thoughts are always occupied with the Lord Jesus— His love, His joy, His peace—then the Holy Spirit will graciously bring the fruit of the Spirit to ripeness within us.

Lord Jesus, teach me this mysterious union between You and the Holy Spirit. May the Spirit so work in me that I will know Your presence in everything I do. Amen.

PRAYING IN THE SPIRIT

And continue to pray as you are directed by the Holy Spirit.
Live in such a way that God's love can bless you.

JUDE 20–21

Paul began the last section of the Epistle to the Ephesians with the words "Be strong with the Lord's mighty power" (Ephesians 6:10). He speaks of the whole armor of God and closes by saying that this armor must be put on with prayer: "Pray at all times and on every occasion in the power of the Holy Spirit" (Ephesians 6:18). Just as we need to be strong in the Lord and wear God's protective armor all day, so we need to live always praying in the Spirit.

The Holy Spirit will not come to us nor work within us just at certain times when we think we need His help. The Spirit comes to be our life-companion. He wants us totally in His possession at all times; otherwise He cannot do His work in us.

When this truth is grasped, we will realize that it is possible to live always praying in the power of the Spirit. The Spirit will keep us in a prayerful attitude and make us realize God's presence. Our prayer will be the continual exercise of fellowship with God and His great love. But as long as we regard the work of the Spirit as restricted to certain times and seasons, it will remain an unsolved mystery and a possible stone of offense.

Holy Spirit, may I know Your blessed nearness which can enable me to abide in Jesus' love at all times. Even in the busiest moments of my life may I pray without ceasing—in entire dependence on You. In Jesus' name, amen.

THE TEMPLE OF GOD

For God's temple is holy,
and you Christians are that temple.

1 CORINTHIANS 3:17

From eternity it was God's desire to create man as a dwelling place through which to show His glory. Because of man's sin, this plan seemed to be a failure. God sought a means of carrying out His plan in His people Israel. He would have a house in the midst of His people—first a tabernacle, and then a temple—in which He could dwell. This was but a shadow of the true indwelling of God in redeemed mankind who would be His temple to eternity.

Since the Holy Spirit has been given, He has His dwelling in each heart that has been cleansed by the Spirit. The message comes to each believer however weak he may be: "Don't you realize that all of you together are the temple of God?" How seldom this truth is experienced; and yet how true it is: "God's temple is holy, and you Christians are that temple."

Paul testified: "Christ lives in me" (Galatians 2:20). This is the fullness of the gospel which he preached: the riches of the glory of the mystery, Christ in you. This is what he prayed for so earnestly for believers: that God would strengthen them through His Spirit in the inner man. Yes, this is what our Lord Himself promised: "All those who love me will do what I say. My Father will love them, and we will come to them and live with them" (John 14:23). Why is it that Christians are so slow to receive this wonder of God's grace?

Lord Jesus, I surrender myself wholly to Your guidance so that I may truly know how to pray. Amen.

THE FELLOWSHIP OF THE SPIRIT

The fellowship of the Holy Spirit be with you all.

2 CORINTHIANS 13:13–14

In this verse we have one of the main characteristics and activities of the Holy Spirit. It is through the Holy Spirit that the Father and Son are one and have fellowship with each other.

We also have fellowship with the Father and the Son through the Spirit. "Our fellowship is with the Father and with his Son, Jesus Christ" (1 John 1:3). "And we know he lives in us because the Holy Spirit lives in us" (1 John 3:24). Through the Spirit we know the fellowship of love with the Father and Son.

Through the Spirit we, as God's children, have fellowship with each other. With the child of God there should be no selfishness. We are members of one Body. Through the Spirit the unity of the Body must be maintained. One reason that the Spirit does not work with greater power in the church is that the unity of the Spirit is not sought after. At Pentecost, after ten days spent in united prayer, the 120 seemed melted together into one body. They received the Spirit in fellowship with each other.

We have the fellowship when we meet at the communion table; we also have fellowship one with another in the trials of other members of the Body. Our text reminds us: "The fellowship of the Holy Spirit be with you all."

In heaven there is an eternal fellowship of love between Father and Son through the Spirit. Do we really long to be filled with the Spirit?

Lord, I offer myself to You, beseeching You to grant me the unity and the fellowship of the Spirit with all members of Christ's Body. In Your name, amen.

WITH THE WHOLE HEART

If you look for me in earnest,
you will find me when you seek me.

JEREMIAH 29:13

I t's often been said that if one seeks to perform any great work, he must do it with his whole heart and with all his might. In business this is the secret of success. Above all in spiritual things it is indispensable, especially in praying for the Holy Spirit.

Let me repeat that the Holy Spirit desires to have full possession of you. He can be satisfied with nothing less if He is to show His full power in your life.

Do you realize when you pray for the Holy Spirit that you are praying for the whole Godhead to take possession of you? Have your prayers had a wrong motive? If you were expecting that God would do something in your heart but in other things you would be free to do your own will, that would be a great mistake. The Holy Spirit must have full possession.

You may not feel a burning, urgent desire for the Holy Spirit to have full control, and you do not see any chance of its becoming true in your life. God knows about this inability of yours; He has ordained that the Holy Spirit will work within you all you need. What God demands of us, He will work within us. On our part there must be earnest prayer each day and an acceptance of the Holy Spirit as our leader.

Child of God, the Holy Spirit longs to possess you wholly. Submit yourself in complete dependence on His promise.

Holy Spirit, even my strongest desires to be controlled by You are not as strong as they should be. Work in me to make my commitment total. I ask in Jesus' name, amen.

THE LOVE OF GOD IN OUR HEARTS

For we know how dearly God loves us,
because he has given us the Holy Spirit
to fill our hearts with his love.

ROMANS 5:5

God the Father fills our hearts with the Holy Spirit. Likewise, the Holy Spirit fills our hearts with the love of God. As truly as God has given us the Spirit, so truly is the love of God given by the Spirit.

Why do we so seldom experience this? Simply because of our unbelief. It takes time to believe in the divine mighty working of the Holy Spirit. We need time to get away from the world and its interests for our souls to rest in the light of God so that the eternal love may take possession of our hearts. If we believe in the infinite love of God and the divine power with which He takes possession of the heart, then we will receive what we ask for—the love of God filling our hearts by the Holy Spirit. God desires His children to love Him with all their hearts and all their strength. He knows that is impossible in our own strength. For that very reason He has given the Spirit to fill our hearts with His love.

If you long for this, draw near to God. Abide with Him in quiet worship and adoration, and you will know the love of God in Christ which passes all knowledge.

Holy Spirit, teach me each day to dwell with the Father in His great love as a little child. Teach me to abide in the love of Christ each day and to show that love toward the church and toward a perishing world. I ask in Christ's name, amen.

WALK IN THE SPIRIT

Live according to your new life in the Holy Spirit. . . .
If we are living now by the Holy Spirit,
let us follow the Holy Spirit's leading in every part of our lives.

GALATIANS 5:16, 25

The Christian in his daily walk must follow the leading of the Spirit. That will be the sign of a spiritual person who serves God in the Spirit and does not trust in his own abilities.

The Spirit is not needed just when we pray or just for our work for God's kingdom. God gives us His Spirit to be in us the whole day. We need Him most in the middle of our daily work because there the world has such power to lead us away from God. We need to ask the Father every morning for a fresh renewal of His Spirit. During the course of the day, let us remind ourselves that the Spirit is with us.

Paul says: "Now, just as you accepted Christ Jesus as your Lord, you must continue to live in obedience to him" (Colossians 2:6). Again: "Put ye on the Lord Jesus Christ" (Romans 13:14 KJV). Just as we put on a coat when we go out, so we must put on the Lord Jesus. We must show by our conduct that Christ lives in us and that we walk by the Spirit.

"Live according to your new life in the Holy Spirit. Then you won't be doing what your sinful nature craves" (Galatians 5:16). If we are not under the guidance of the Holy Spirit, we will do things in our own strength. The Spirit is given to teach us that we may walk by the Spirit at all times.

Thank You, God, for this divine Leader who gives us daily renewal from heaven and enables us to walk and to abide in Christ. In Your name, amen.

THE SPIRIT PROMISED
TO THE OBEDIENT

"If you love me, obey my commandments.
And I will ask the Father,
and he will give you another Counselor,
who will never leave you."

JOHN 14:15–16

Christ would ascend to heaven and ask the Father to send the Comforter, the Holy Spirit. He would not do this only once, but it would become part of His intercessory work. He would "live forever to plead with God on their behalf" (Hebrews 7:25).

The Lord tells us in John 14 on what conditions He will send the Spirit: if we love Him and keep His commandments, "I will ask the Father." The Holy Spirit is given to enable us to do the will of the Father. The conditions are reasonable and just. As we keep the commandments through the Spirit, the Spirit will be granted to us in fuller measure. Let us say to God that we will strive to keep His commands.

Do not listen to the whispers of Satan or give way to unbelief. Surrender yourself unreservedly to the Lord, who has said: "If you love me, obey my commandments." Love will enable you to do it. Trust the Lord Jesus with childlike faith and give yourself completely to do His will—that is all that is necessary. Then the beauty of the divine agreement that He makes with us will become reality: "When you obey me, you remain in my love. . ." (John 15:10). The Father will send the Holy Spirit anew each day.

Lord Jesus, I love You. I trust You to ask the Father to send the Holy Spirit to live in me daily. Amen.

THE SPIRIT OF WISDOM

I pray for you constantly, asking God. . .
to give you spiritual wisdom and understanding,
so that you might grow in your knowledge of God.

EPHESIANS 1:16–17

In the Word of God we find a wonderful combination of the human and the divine. Anyone who has a good understanding of language can grasp the meaning of the words and the truths contained in them. But this is all that can be done in the power of human understanding.

There is a divine side in which the holy God expresses His deepest thoughts to us. We cannot understand them or comprehend them, for they must be spiritually discerned. Only through the Holy Spirit can the Christian apply the divine truth contained in God's Word.

Much of our religion is ineffectual because people accept the truths of God's Word with their intellect and strive to put them into practice in their own strength. Even a young student in a theological seminary may accept the truths of God's Word as head knowledge, but the Word has little power in his heart to lead to a life of joy and peace in the Lord Jesus. Paul teaches us that when we read God's Word we should pray, "Father, give me spiritual wisdom and understanding." As we do this each day we will find that God's Word is living and powerful and will work in our hearts and lives.

Father, I echo Paul's prayer, "Give me spiritual wisdom and understanding." I desire Your Word to be living and powerful in my life, and I request this in Jesus' name, amen.

THE SPIRIT OF SANCTIFICATION

God the Father chose you long ago,
and the Spirit has made you holy.
As a result, you have obeyed Jesus Christ
and are cleansed by his blood.

1 PETER 1:2

In the New Testament the word "holy" is attributed to the Holy Spirit. Christ set Himself apart for us that we might be holy. The great work of the Holy Spirit is to glorify Christ in us by purifying us.

Have you really understood this truth? The main object for which the Holy Spirit is given is to purify you! If you do not accept this truth, then the Holy Spirit cannot do His cleansing work. If you only want the Spirit to help you to be a little better and to pray a little more, you will not get very far. But when you understand that the Holy Spirit was given in order to impart God's holiness and will cleanse you completely, then you will begin to realize that the Holy Spirit dwells in your heart.

And what will be the result? You will want Him to be in complete control of your life each day.

Your whole life and conversation must be in the Spirit. Your prayer, your faith, your fellowship with the Father, and all your work in God's service must be completely under His control. As the Spirit of holiness, He is the Spirit of your purification.

This is a deep, eternal truth. But it will be of no consequence if we do not wait upon God to grant us the Spirit of divine wisdom and a vision of what God has intended for us—the Spirit of purification. Each morning pray:

"Abba, Father, for this new day renew within me the gift of Your Holy Spirit. Amen."

RIVERS OF LIVING WATER

"If you believe in me, come and drink!
For the Scriptures declare that rivers of living water
will flow out from within."

JOHN 7:38

Jesus, in His conversation with the Samaritan woman, said: "The water I give them takes away thirst altogether. It becomes a perpetual spring within them, giving them eternal life" (John 4:14). In John 7:38 the promise is even greater: rivers of living waters flowing from him, bringing life and blessing to others. John says that this refers to the Holy Spirit, who would come when Christ had been glorified.

What do we need in order to experience the rivers of living water? Just one thing: the inner connection to Christ—the unreserved surrender to fellowship with Him. We have the firm assurance that His Spirit will work in us what we cannot do. We need a faith that rejoices in the divine power and love. We need a faith that depends on Him day by day to grant us grace that living water may flow out from us.

If the water from a reservoir is to flow into a house all day, one thing is necessary: The connection must be perfect. Then the water passes through the pipe of its own accord. So the connection between us and Christ must be uninterrupted. Our faith must accept Christ and depend on Him to sustain the new life.

Lord God, I rejoice that Jesus Christ gives us the Holy Spirit! Thank You for the assurance that the Holy Spirit is within me as a fountain of blessing. I pray in Jesus' name, amen.

JOY IN GOD

For the Kingdom of God is not a matter of
what we eat or drink,
but of living a life of goodness and peace
and joy in the Holy Spirit.

ROMANS 14:17

A Christian man said to me shortly after his conversion: "I always thought that if I became religious, it would be impossible for me to do my worldly business. The two things seemed so contrary. I seemed to be a man trying to dig a vineyard with a bag of sand on his shoulders. But when I found the Lord I was so filled with joy that I could do my work cheerfully from morning 'til night. The bag of sand was gone; the joy of the Lord was my strength."

Many Christians do not understand that the joy of the Lord will keep them and enable them for their work. Read the Scriptures and see how the kingdom of God is pure joy and peace through the Holy Spirit. God will "keep you happy and full of peace as you believe in him. . .through the power of the Holy Spirit."

Then try to realize that the Holy Spirit will give this joy and peace of Christ in our hearts. It is wrong to think of the Holy Spirit as a matter of grief and self-reproach, of disappointment, of something too high and holy. The great gift of the Father is meant to keep us in the joy and peace of Christ.

Listen attentively to the voice of the Spirit each day as He points to Jesus Christ, who offers you His wonderful fruit: love, joy, peace.

Holy Spirit, I come to You in humility believing firmly that You will lead me into the joy of the Lord. I willingly follow You. Amen.

All the Day — Every Day

I will bless you every day.

PSALM 145:2

It is a step forward in the Christian life when you seek to have fellowship with God in His Word each day without fail. Perseverance will be crowned with success if you are really sincere. The experience may be somewhat as follows:

When you wake up in the morning, God will be your first thought. Set apart a time for prayer and resolve to give God time to hear requests and to reveal Himself. You may share all your desires with God and expect an answer.

Later on in the day, even if only for a few minutes, take time to keep up the fellowship with God. And again in the evening take time to reflect on the day's work and, with confession of sin, receive the assurance of forgiveness. Then commit yourself anew to God and His service.

Gradually you will get an insight into what is lacking in life and will be ready for uninterrupted fellowship with God through the Holy Spirit. You will gain the assurance through faith that the Holy Spirit, the Lord Jesus, and the Father Himself will give His presence and help all through the day.

Remember that you only need to live life one day at a time. You don't have to worry about tomorrow but rest in the assurance that He who has led you today will be even closer tomorrow.

Lord God, grant me the perseverance to spend time each day with You in Your Word and in prayer. In Jesus' name, amen.

THE SPIRIT AND THE CROSS

For by the power of the eternal Spirit,
Christ offered himself to God as a perfect sacrifice for our sins.

HEBREWS 9:14

The connection between the cross and the Spirit is incon-
ceivably close and meaningful. The Spirit brought Christ
to the cross and enabled Him to die there. The cross gave Christ
the right to bring down the Holy Spirit on earth because there
He made reconciliation for sin. The cross gave Christ the right
and the power to grant us the power of the Spirit because on it
He set us free from the power of sin.

Christ could not have attained to the heavenly life, or
poured out the Holy Spirit, if He had not first died to sin, to
the world, and to His own life. He died to sin that He might
live to God. And that is the way the Holy Spirit brings the
cross into our hearts. It is only as we have been crucified with
Christ that we can receive the full power of the Spirit. When
we do not realize how necessary it is to die to all earthly things,
the Spirit cannot gain full possession of us.

If we as Christians rely only on our human understanding,
we cannot understand or experience that the fellowship of the
Spirit is a fellowship of the cross. Wait on God to teach you
divine truths through the Spirit.

God, grant me a vision of how the Spirit will take me to the cross of
Christ to die to the world and to sin so that all things may become
new. Then I will actually live and work and pray in the Spirit to Your
glory. Amen.

THE SPIRIT AND THE BLOOD

So we have these three witnesses—
the Spirit, the water, and the blood—
and all three agree.

1 JOHN 5:7–8

B aptism by water is an external sign of inner renewing and
purifying through regeneration. The Spirit and the blood
are spiritual expressions, working together in regeneration: the
blood for the forgiveness of sins, the Spirit for the renewal of
the whole nature.

There is spiritual oneness in the Spirit and the blood.
Through the blood we obtain the Spirit, as through the blood we
are redeemed and purified to receive the Spirit. Only through the
blood can we pray with confidence to receive the Spirit.

There may be some sin in your life of which you are hardly
conscious but which grieves the Spirit and drives Him away.
The only way to avoid this is to believe that "the blood of Jesus,
his Son, cleanses us from every sin" (1 John 1:7). Your only right
to approach God is through the blood of the Lamb. Come with
every sin, known or unknown, and plead the blood of Christ as
your only claim to forgiveness.

But do not be content with just the forgiveness of sins.
Accept the fullness of the Spirit which comes by the blood of
Christ. Do not for a moment doubt that you have a right
through the blood to the fullness of the Spirit.

As one who has been redeemed by the blood, give yourself
to God as His purchased possession—a vessel ready for Him to
use, a dwelling-place of the Holy Spirit.

Lord Jesus, thank You for shedding Your blood to pay the price for my
sin so that I can have the Holy Spirit. Amen.

THE SPIRIT IN PREACHER AND HEARER

For when we brought you the Good News,
it was not only with words but also with power. . . .
So you received the message with joy from the Holy Spirit.

1 THESSALONIANS 1:5–6

Paul more than once reminds his converts that the chief characteristic of his preaching was the supernatural power of the Holy Spirit. This is one of the most important lessons in the spiritual life. We as hearers are accustomed to listening attentively to the sermon to see what it has to teach us. But we may forget that the blessing of our churchgoing depends on two things. First, it depends on the prayer for the preacher that "the Holy Spirit [will be] powerful"; then prayer for ourselves that we may receive the word not from people, but as God's Word, which "continues to work in you who believe" (1 Thessalonians 2:13). How often there is no manifestation of the Spirit when both the speaking and the hearing are mainly the work of human understanding or feeling.

We should pray earnestly that God will reveal to both minister and people "spiritual wisdom and understanding" (Ephesians 1:17) that we may discover what place the Holy Spirit really should have in our lives. As God gives us wisdom we will understand what Christ meant when He said: " 'Do not leave Jerusalem until the Father sends you what he promised. . . . But when the Holy Spirit has come upon you, you will receive power and will tell people about me everywhere. . .to the ends of the earth' " (Acts 1:4, 8).

Dear Jesus, teach us to pray down the power of the Holy Spirit upon ministers and missionaries and their congregations. May the preaching be in the manifestation of the Spirit and of power for the conversion and cleansing of souls. In Your name, amen.

THE FULL GOSPEL

"You must turn from your sins and turn to God,
and be baptized in the name of Jesus Christ. . . .
Then you will receive the gift of the Holy Spirit."

ACTS 2:38

When John the Baptist preached, "Turn from your sins and turn to God, because the Kingdom of Heaven is near" (Matthew 4:17), he also said: "Someone is coming soon who is greater than I am. . . . He will baptize you with the Holy Spirit and with fire" (Luke 3:16). When Christ preached the gospel of the kingdom, He said: "And I assure you that some of you standing here right now will not die before you see me, the Son of Man, coming in my Kingdom" (Matthew 16:28). This is what happened at the outpouring of the Holy Spirit.

Peter preached on the Day of Pentecost the full gospel of repentance, forgiveness of sins, and the gift of the Holy Spirit. This is indispensable in preaching the gospel, for only then is it possible for a Christian to live in the will of God and to please Him in all things. The continuous joy of which Christ speaks can only be obtained through the power of the Holy Spirit.

How often only half the gospel is preached—conversion and forgiveness of sins. The appropriation of the life of the Spirit is not mentioned. No wonder so many Christians fail to understand that they must depend each day on the Spirit.

Accept this truth for yourself. The daily enjoyment of the leading of God's Spirit is indispensable for a joyous life of faith. Ask the Father to grant you the gift of the Holy Spirit anew each day.

Father, thank You that You have given the full gospel, not only of repentance and new life in Christ, but also of the power of the Holy Spirit. Grant to me each day the Holy Spirit. In Jesus' name, amen.

The Ministry of the Spirit

Clearly, you are a letter from Christ prepared by us.
It is written not with pen and ink,
but with the Spirit of the living God.
It is carved not on stone, but on human hearts.

2 Corinthians 3:3

The Corinthians' church was a "letter of recommendation" for Paul, showing how much he had done for them. Although he claimed nothing for himself, God had enabled him as a "minister of the Spirit" to write in their hearts "with the Spirit of the living God."

What a wonderful example of the work of a minister for his people! A preacher prepared to be a minister of the Spirit, with power to write in the hearts of his people the name and the love of Christ. No wonder Paul speaks of how "all of us have had that veil removed so that we can be mirrors that brightly reflect the glory of the Lord. And as the Spirit of the Lord works within us, we become more and more like him and reflect his glory even more" (2 Corinthians 3:18).

May God restore the ministry of the gospel to its original power! If only ministers and church members would unite in the prayer that God, by the working of His Spirit, would give the ministry of the Spirit its right place. We need to pray that God will teach the people to believe that when Christ is preached to them, they are seeing as in a mirror the glory of the Lord and may be changed into the same image by the Spirit of the Lord!

O Lord, help us to persevere in the prayer that the Holy Spirit may again have His rightful place in the ministry of the Word, so that the exceeding and abundant glory of this ministry may be manifested. For Jesus' sake, amen.

THE SPIRIT FROM HEAVEN

*And now this Good News has been announced
by those who preached to you in the power of
the Holy Spirit sent from heaven.*

1 PETER 1:12

C hrist has taught us to think of God as our own Father in heaven who is ready to give His blessings to His children on earth. Our Lord Himself was taken up into the glory of heaven, and we are told that we are seated with Him in the heavenly places in Christ. The Holy Spirit comes to us from heaven to fill our hearts with the light, the love, the joy, and the power of heaven.

Those who are truly filled with the Spirit have a heavenly life in themselves. They are in daily fellowship with the Father and with the Son and seek the things that are above. Their main characteristic is heavenly-mindedness. They carry with them the marks of their eternal, heavenly destiny.

How can we cultivate this heavenly disposition? By allowing the Holy Spirit, sent from heaven, to do His heavenly work in our hearts and to bring to maturity in our lives the fruit of the Spirit. The Spirit will lift our hearts to daily fellowship with God in heaven. The Spirit makes the glorified Christ in heaven present in our hearts and teaches us to dwell in His presence.

Father, may I take time each day to receive from You the continual guidance of the Holy Spirit. Let Him overcome the world for me and strengthen me as a child of heaven to walk daily with You and with the Lord Jesus. I ask in Jesus' name, amen.

THE SPIRIT AND PRAYER

"The truth is,
you can go directly to the Father and ask him,
and he will grant your request because you use my name."

JOHN 16:23

In Jesus' farewell discourse (John 13–17), He presented life in the Spirit in all its power and attractiveness. Through the Holy Spirit God's children can go directly to the Father and ask God to bless the world. Seven times we have the promise repeated: "You can ask for anything in my name, and I will do it" (John 14:13–14; 15:7, 16; 16:23–24, 26). Read these passages over so that you may come to understand how urgently and earnestly our Lord repeated the promise.

During the ten days before Pentecost the disciples proved this. In response to their continuous united prayer, the heavens were opened. The Spirit of God descended to earth, filling them with His life. They received the power of the Spirit that they might impart it to thousands. That power is still the pledge of what God will do. If God's children will agree with one accord to wait for the promise of the Father each day, there is no limit to what God will do for them.

Christian, remember that the Holy Spirit will dwell in you with divine power, enabling you to testify for Him. But it also means that you may unite with God's children to ask in prayer greater and more wonderful things than the heart can imagine.

Dear Lord, it is almost too wonderful to me to know that, whatever I desire in Jesus' name, He will do for me. I praise and thank You for this glorious gift. Amen.

WITH ONE ACCORD IN PRAYER

They all met together continually for prayer.

ACTS 1:14

J esus gave the command to His disciples: "Go into all the world and preach the Good News to everyone, everywhere" (Mark 16:15). He added the promise: "And be sure of this: I am with you always" (Matthew 28:20). This command and this promise were not meant only for the disciples but also for us.

Before His ascension Christ gave His last command with a promise. The command was: "Do not leave Jerusalem until the Father sends you what he promised" (Acts 1:4). The promise was: "When the Holy Spirit has come upon you, you will receive power and will tell people about me everywhere. . .to the ends of the earth" (Acts 1:8). This command and promise are also meant for us. As irrevocable as the command to preach the gospel is the command to wait for the Father to send what He promised—"When the Holy Spirit has come upon you, you will receive power."

For ten days the disciples pled in one accord and their prayer was answered. The Church of our day has tried to carry out the first command to preach the gospel, but it has often forgotten the second command to wait for the Father to send what He promised. The power of the first disciples lay in the fact that they, as one body, were prepared to forget themselves and to pray for the Holy Spirit.

Whatever you may have learned from reading this book, learn one more lesson. Daily prayer in fellowship with God's children is indispensable if the Spirit is again to come in power. Pray for power.

Dear Lord, in Jesus' name I ask for the gift of Your Holy Spirit on me and on all the Church so that in unity we may do Your work and demonstrate Your love. Amen.

PRAY AT ALL TIMES

*Pray at all times and on every occasion
in the power of the Holy Spirit.
Stay alert and be persistent in your prayers
for all Christians everywhere.
And pray for me, too.*

EPHESIANS 6:18–19

P ray at all times. Who can do this? How can we do it when we are surrounded by the cares of daily life? How can a mother love her child at all times? I can breathe and feel and hear at all times because all these are the functions of a healthy, natural life. If our spiritual life is healthy, under the power of the Holy Spirit, praying at all times will be natural.

Pray at all times. Does it refer to continual acts of prayer, in which we are to persevere until we receive an answer, or to the spirit of prayerfulness that should animate us all day? It includes both. Jesus gives us an example of this. We have to spend special times of prayer in private. We are also to walk all day in God's presence with our focus on heavenly things. Without set times of prayer the spirit of prayer will be dull. Without the continual prayerfulness the set times will not be effective.

Pray at all times. Does it refer to prayer for ourselves or for others? It refers to both, but too often we confine it to ourselves.

The death of Christ brought Him to the place of everlasting intercession. Our death with Him to sin and self sets us free from selfishness and elevates us to the dignity of intercessor— one who can get life and blessing from God for others.

Father, help me to know my calling and give myself wholly to it. May I find prayer always within me. In Jesus' name, amen.

Becoming Educated

I urge you. . .to pray for all people.
As you make your requests, plead for God's mercy upon them,
and give thanks. Pray this way for. . .all. . .who are in authority.

1 TIMOTHY 2:1–2

Pray without ceasing. How can we learn to do that? The best way of learning to do a thing—in fact the only way—is to do it. Begin by setting apart some time every day, say ten or fifteen minutes, in which you say to God and to yourself that you come to Him now as intercessor for others. It can be in the morning, in the evening, or any other time. Do not worry if you cannot set aside the same time every day. Just see that you do it. Christ chose you and appointed you to pray for others.

If at first you do not feel any special urgency, faith, or power in your prayers, do not let that hinder you. Quietly tell the Lord Jesus of your weakness. Believe that the Holy Spirit is in you to teach you to pray. Be assured that, if you begin, God will help you. God cannot help you unless you begin and keep on.

Pray at all times. How do I know what to pray for? Once you begin to think of all the needs around you, you will soon find enough to pray for. But to help you, each day for the next few weeks we will concentrate on subjects and hints for prayer. Use and reuse these ideas until you know more fully to follow the Spirit's leading and have learned, if need be, to make your own list of subjects. These days can be a time of becoming educated in this matter of praying at all times.

Lord, I am looking forward to learning more of You and how to pray. Please be my teacher. In Jesus' name, amen.

How to Pray

The Holy Spirit prays for us with groanings
that cannot be expressed in words.

ROMANS 8:26

If only topics for prayer were given, one might fall into the routine of mentioning names and things before God and prayer would become a burden. Therefore "how to pray" hints are included. They are meant to remind us of the spiritual nature of prayer and of the need for divine help. They will encourage our faith in the certainty that God, through the Spirit, will give us grace to pray and will also hear our prayer. It takes time to learn to pray with boldness and to dare to believe that you will be heard.

Take a few moments each day to listen to God's voice reminding you of how certainly even you will be heard. Listen to Him calling you to pray with faith in your Father and to claim and take the blessing you plead for. Let these words about how to pray enter your hearts and thoughts at other times, too. The work of intercession is one of Christ's great works on earth, entrusted to Him because He gave Himself a sacrifice to God for us. The work of intercession is the greatest work a Christian can do. Give yourself as a sacrifice to God for others, and intercession will become your glory and your joy, too.

Lord Jesus, I have a lot to learn about prayer. May I not just learn facts. May the lessons You have in store for me truly become lessons that my very heart learns. Amen.

WHAT TO PRAY

Pray for each other.

JAMES 5:16

Scripture calls us to pray for many things: for all Christians, for all men and women, for all in government, and for all who are in adversity. It tells us to pray for sending missionaries, for those in the ministry of the gospel, for believers who have fallen into sin, for those in our own circle of friends. The Church is now much larger than when the New Testament was written. The number of ministries and workers is much greater. The needs of the Church and the world are so much better known that we must take time to see where prayer is needed and to what our heart is most drawn.

The scriptural calls to prayer demand a large heart, taking in all saints, and all men and women, and all needs. An attempt will be made these next days to indicate what the chief subjects are that need prayer and that ought to interest every Christian.

It may be difficult to pray for such large spheres as are sometimes mentioned. Where one subject appears of more special interest or more urgent than another, spend some time day after day to pray about that. If you really give time to intercession and the spirit of believing intercession is cultivated, the object is accomplished. While the heart must be enlarged at times to take in all, the more pointed and definite our prayer can be, the better.

Father, may this adventure of learning more about what to pray for result in a renewed relationship with You and with those for whom I pray. Amen.

ANSWERS TO PRAYER

Do not leave. . .
until the Father sends you what he promised.

ACTS 1:4

W hen we pray for all believers, or for missions in general, it is difficult to know when or how our prayer is answered, or whether our prayer had any part in bringing the answer. To remind us that God hears us, we should take note of what answers we look for and when they come. On the day of praying for all believers, take those in your congregation or in your prayer group and ask for a revival among them. In connection with missions, take some special location or missionary you are interested in and pray for blessing. Record definite requests with regard to individuals or special areas and look for the answers. Expect and look for God's answers so that you may praise Him.

When committing to persistent, meaningful prayer—prayer that expects answers—it may be helpful to have a small prayer group. You may meet for prayer once a month with some special topic introduced for every day. You may meet for a year or longer with the aim of strengthening each other in the grace of intercession. If you were to invite some of your believing friends to join for some special requests along with printed topics for prayer, or to unite in prayer for revival, some might join you in the great privilege of intercession who now stand idle because no one has invited them.

Lord, thank You for answering prayer. I praise You for Your desire to respond to our prayers. Amen.

GOD IS SUFFICIENT

My gracious favor is all you need.

2 CORINTHIANS 12:9

Who is sufficient for real intercession? The more we study and try to practice the grace of intercession, the more we feel overwhelmed by its greatness and our weakness. Let that feeling lead you to hear: "My gracious favor is all you need," and to answer truthfully, "Our only power and success come from God" (2 Corinthians 3:5).

Take courage; you are called to take part in the intercession of Christ. The burden and the agony, the triumph and the victory, are all His. Learn from Him; to know how to pray, yield to His Spirit in you. He gave Himself as a sacrifice to God for us that He might have the right and power of intercession. "He bore the sins of many and interceded for sinners" (Isaiah 53:12).

Let your faith rest boldly on His finished work. Let your heart identify with Him in His death and His life. Like Him, give yourself to God a sacrifice for others. It is your highest calling, your true and full union with Him.

Come and give your whole heart and life to intercession, and you will know its blessedness and its power. God asks nothing less; the world needs nothing less; Christ asks nothing less; let nothing less be what we offer to God.

All sufficient God, I turn to You in recognition of my insufficiency. Be my sufficiency as I pray. Enable me to be the intercessor that You desire. Amen.

THE POWER OF THE HOLY SPIRIT

I pray that. . .
he will give you mighty inner strength
through his Holy Spirit.

EPHESIANS 3:16

P ray for the full manifestation of the grace and energy of the Holy Spirit to remove all that is contrary to God's revealed will. Do this so that we do not grieve the Holy Spirit. Then He can work with mightier power in the Church for the exaltation of Christ and for our blessing.

All prayer unites in the one request—the power of the Holy Spirit. Make it your prayer. Pray as a child asks a father. "You fathers—if your children ask for a fish, do you give them a snake? . . .If you sinful people know how to give good gifts to your children, how much more will your heavenly Father give the Holy Spirit to those who ask him" (Luke 11:11, 13).

Ask as simply and trustfully as a child asks for food. You can do this because "God has sent the Spirit of his Son into your hearts, and now you can call God your dear Father" (Galatians 4:6). This Spirit is in you to give you childlike confidence. Have faith in the fact that He is praying in you. In that faith ask for the power of the Holy Spirit everywhere. Mention places or groups where you especially desire it to be seen.

Dear Lord, I am Your child and I come to You knowing that You love me. Fill me with Your Holy Spirit and may His power be demonstrated in the life and work of Your Church. In Jesus' name, amen.

THE SPIRIT OF PRAYER

"I will pour out a spirit of grace and prayer."

ZECHARIAH 12:10

The evangelization of the world depends first of all upon a revival of prayer. It is needed more than personal witness or missionaries. Deep down at the bottom of our spiritless life is the need for the forgotten secret of persistent, worldwide prayer.

Every child of God has the Holy Spirit in him to pray. God waits to give you the Spirit in full measure.

Pray in the Spirit as Paul taught us: "Pray at all times and on every occasion in the power of the Holy Spirit" (Ephesians 6:18). Jude also wrote: "Continue to pray as you are directed by the Holy Spirit" (Jude 20).

On His resurrection day our Lord gave His disciples the Holy Spirit to enable them to wait for the full outpouring on the day of Pentecost. It is only as we acknowledge and yield to the power of the Spirit already in us that we can pray for His full manifestation.

Father, Your love is so endless, so mighty, so willing to take possession of me. Let that love have full sway in my heart. Draw me to Yourself that I will continue in prayer and delight in fellowship with You until You take full control. Fill me with the desire and the power to pray for this world. Amen.

PRAY FOR ALL SAINTS

Pray at all times and on every occasion
in the power of the Holy Spirit.
Stay alert and be persistent in your prayers
for all Christians everywhere.

EPHESIANS 6:18

E very member of a body is interested in the welfare of the whole and exists to help and complete the others. Believers are one body and ought to pray, not so much for the welfare of their own church, but for all saints. This large, unselfish love is proof that Christ's Spirit and love are teaching us to pray. Pray first for all believers and then for those around you.

Pray in the love of the Spirit. Jesus said, "Your love for one another will prove to the world that you are my disciples" (John 13:35). He taught us that we are to have the unity that comes from love. " 'My prayer for all of them is that they will be one. . . and the world will believe you sent me' " (John 17:21).

Paul taught us to pray from love. "Dear friends, I urge you in the name of our Lord Jesus Christ to join me in my struggle by praying to God for me. Do this because of your love for me, given to you by the Holy Spirit" (Romans 15:30). And Paul's teaching was reinforced by Peter. "Most important of all, continue to show deep love for each other. . ." (1 Peter 4:8).

If we are to pray, we must love.

Father, I love all Your children, especially those I know. Where my love falls short may Your Holy Spirit pray for me. Let His love take full possession of me. Help me pray with the fervent love of the Spirit. May Your love become mine so that I may yield myself to live wholeheartedly in and for that love. In Jesus' name, amen.

THE SPIRIT OF HOLINESS

"Make them pure and holy by teaching them your words of truth."

JOHN 17:17

God is the Holy One. His people are a holy people. He speaks: "I, the Lord, am holy, and I make you holy" (Leviticus 21:8). Christ prayed: " 'Make them pure and holy by teaching them your words of truth' " (John 17:17). Paul prayed: "Christ will make your hearts strong, blameless, and holy when you stand before God. . ." (1 Thessalonians 3:13). "May the God of peace make you holy in every way" (1 Thessalonians 5:23).

Pray for all the believers—God's holy ones—throughout the Church. Pray that the Spirit of holiness may rule them. Especially pray for new converts. Pray for the believers in your own neighborhood or congregation, especially for any you are interested in. Think of their special need, weakness, or sin, and pray that God may make them holy.

Pray, trusting in God's omnipotence. The things that are impossible with men are possible with God. Often when we ask for great things, we think there is little likelihood of their happening. Prayer is not only wishing or asking, but believing and accepting. Be still before God and ask Him to allow you to know Him as the Almighty One and leave your requests with Him who does wonders.

Lord, hear my prayer for the people of my own church. Hear my prayer for men and women in Your Church all over the world. O God, let Your light shine forth and Your glory be upon them, that they may experience Your holiness. In Jesus' name, amen.

KEPT FROM THE WORLD

*"Holy Father, keep them and care for them. . . .
I'm not asking you to take them out of the world,
but to keep them safe from the evil one."*

JOHN 17:11, 15

Pray that God's people may be kept from the world. The night before He was crucified, Christ asked three things for His disciples: (1) that they might be kept and cared for as those who are not of the world; (2) that they might be purified; (3) that they might be one in love. You cannot do better than to pray just as Jesus prayed. Ask that God's people may be kept separate from the world and the evil one. Pray that they, by the Holy Spirit, may live as those who are not of the world.

Pray with confidence before God. "Dear friends, if our conscience is clear, we can come to God with bold confidence. And we will receive whatever we request because we obey him and do the things that please him" (1 John 3:21–22).

Memorize that verse. Get the words into your heart. Join the ranks of those who, like John, draw near to God with an assured heart that does not condemn them. Learn to have confidence toward God. In the quiet confidence of an obedient child, pray for those believers who sin (1 John 5:16). Pray for all to be kept from the evil one. And say often, "What we ask, we receive, because we keep and do."

Lord, may we your people be kept from the world, bowing only to Your lordship and not to the god of this world. Glorify Yourself in the life of Your Church made holy by Your Spirit. Amen.

The Spirit of Love in the Church

When the Holy Spirit controls our lives,
he will produce this kind of fruit in us: love. . . .

Galatians 5:22

T hat they may be one, as we are—I in them and you in me.
. . . Then the world will know that you sent me and will
understand that you love them as much as you love me. . .that
your love for me may be in them and I in them'" (John
17:22–23, 26). Believers are one in Christ, as He is one with the
Father. The love of God rests on them and can dwell in them.
Pray that the power of the Holy Spirit will put this love in
believers so that the world may see and know God's love in
them. Pray consistently for this.

Pray as one of God's reminders: "I have posted watchmen
on your walls; they will pray to the Lord day and night for the
fulfillment of his promises. Take no rest, all you who pray"
(Isaiah 62:6).

Study these words until your whole soul is filled with the
realization: I am appointed as an intercessor. Enter God's presence with that faith. Approach the world's need with this
thought: It is my job to intercede. Meditate on the fact that the
Holy Spirit will teach you how to pray and what to pray for. Let
it be a constant awareness: My great life work, like Christ's, is
intercession. My purpose is to pray for believers and those who
still do not know God.

Lord God, I count it a high privilege to know that I am appointed an
intercessor. I also know it is a great responsibility. Enable me to inter-
cede in the power of Your Spirit. Amen.

THE HOLY SPIRIT AND MINISTERS

I urge you. . .
to join me in my struggle by praying to God for me.

ROMANS 15:30

Paul and Timothy emphasized their need for prayer as ministers of Christ. "He will rescue us because you are helping by praying for us" (2 Corinthians 1:11). There are a lot of ministers in Christ's Church and they need prayer. They would have a mighty ministry if they were all covered with the power of the Holy Spirit. Pray for this in earnest. Think of your own minister and ask for the Holy Spirit's power especially for him. Ask that ministers everywhere be filled with the Spirit. Plead for them the promise, "Stay here. . .until the Holy Spirit comes and fills you with power from heaven" (Luke 24:49). "When the Holy Spirit has come upon you, you will receive power. . ." (Acts 1:8).

Pray in private. "When you pray, go away by yourself, shut the door behind you, and pray to your Father secretly" (Matthew 6:6). Jesus "went up into the hills by himself to pray" (Matthew 14:23; see John 6:15).

Take time to be alone with God to intercede for His servants. Don't think that you have no influence or that your prayers don't count. Your prayer and your faith will make a difference. Go away by yourself and pray to God for His ministers.

Lord, I want a special place in my world for secret prayer, a place where I can regularly remember my pastor and all who follow You. Enable me to spend a regular time in secret prayer. Amen.

CHRISTIAN WORKERS

He will rescue us because
you are helping by praying for us.

2 CORINTHIANS 1:11

There are multitudes of Christian workers ministering in connection with our churches and missions, schools and colleges, our publishers and bookstores, our public service and government offices, young men and young women, children and youth, our worship in music, our military personnel, hospitals and clinics, prisons, and our poor. Praise God for this! How much more they could accomplish if each were living in the fullness of the Holy Spirit! Pray for them; it makes you a partner in their work. You will praise God each time you hear of blessings anywhere.

Pray with definite requests. Jesus asked the blind beggar, "What do you want me to do for you?" (Luke 18:41). The Lord knew what the man wanted, and yet He asked him. Verbalizing our wish gives meaning to our transaction with God. It awakens faith and expectation.

Being definite in your requests also helps you to know what answer you are looking for. Ask those you are praying for what they need. If they have prayer letters, use them as guides. Intercession is not mere words and pious wishes. Its aim is to receive and bring down blessing through believing, persevering prayer.

Father, thank You for those who serve You as Christian workers. I pray for those I know personally and for all of them throughout the world. May they know the power of Your Spirit. Amen.

MISSION WORK

One day as these men were worshiping the Lord and fasting,
the Holy Spirit said,
"Dedicate Barnabas and Saul for
the special work I have for them."

ACTS 13:2

The evangelization of the world depends, first of all, upon a revival of prayer. The need for the forgotten secret of prevailing, worldwide prayer is greater than the need for missionaries.

Pray that our missions work may all be done in this spirit: waiting on God, hearing the voice of the Spirit, sending out men and women with fasting and prayer. Pray that in our churches our mission interests may be in the power of the Holy Spirit and of prayer. It is a Spirit-filled, praying church that will send out Spirit-filled missionaries, mighty in prayer.

Take time when you pray. The psalmist said, "I give myself unto prayer" (Psalm 109:4, KJV). The early church leaders agreed. "We can spend our time in prayer" (Acts 6:4). Solomon in his God-given wisdom said, "Don't make rash promises to God. . . . Let your words be few" (Ecclesiastes 5:2).

Time is one of the main standards to measure value. The time we give is proof of the interest we feel. We need time with God—to know His presence and to wait for Him to make Himself known. We need time to consider and feel the needs we pray for. We need time to pray until we can believe that we have received.

Holy Spirit, I pray for all missionaries that they may know the close-
ness, the fullness, the power of Your Spirit as they serve You. In Jesus'
name, amen.

MISSIONARIES

When the Holy Spirit has come upon you,
you will receive power and will tell people about me everywhere.

ACTS 1:8

Missionaries today need an outpouring of God's Spirit in their lives and ministries. God always gives His servants power equal to the work He asks of them. There are difficult times in this work of casting out Satan from his strongholds. Pray that everyone who takes part in it may receive and act in the power of the Holy Spirit. Think of the specific difficulties of your missionaries and pray for them.

Pray, trusting in God's faithfulness. "God can be trusted to keep his promise. . . . [Sarah] believed that God would keep his promise" (Hebrews 10:23; 11:11).

Just think about God's promises to His Son concerning His kingdom, His promises to the Church concerning the unbelievers, and His promises to His servants concerning their work. Think of His promises to you concerning your prayer. Then pray in the assurance that He is faithful and only waits for prayer and faith to fulfill them. "God, who calls you" (to pray), "is faithful; he will do this" (what He has promised) (1 Thessalonians 5:24).

Pray for individual missionaries, making yourself one with them, until you know that you are heard. Begin to live for Christ's kingdom as the one thing worth living for!

Father, I pray for Your children throughout the whole world, particularly for those missionaries who are doing Your work. Fill them for their task. In Jesus' name, amen.

MORE WORKERS

*"So pray to the Lord who is in charge of the harvest;
ask him to send out more workers for his fields."*

MATTHEW 9:38

It is remarkable that Jesus seeks help from His disciples in getting the need for workers supplied. What an honor put upon prayer. It is also proof that God wants prayer and will hear it.

Pray for students in theological seminaries and Bible schools that God will prepare them and send them out. Pray that all believers may be ready to go or to pray for those who go.

Pray by faith, doubting nothing. "Jesus said to the disciples, 'Have faith in God. I assure you that you can say to this mountain, "May God lift you up and throw you into the sea," and your command will be obeyed. All that's required is that you really believe and do not doubt in your heart'" (Mark 11:22–23).

Have faith in God! Ask Him to make Himself known to you as the faithful, mighty God. You will be encouraged to believe that He can give suitable and sufficient workers however impossible this seems. But remember, He does so in answer to prayer and faith.

Apply this to every opening where a good worker is needed. The work is God's. He can give the right person, but He must be asked.

Lord Jesus, put on the hearts of those You have chosen the desire to forsake all and follow You wherever You lead. Let Your Church take up the task of praying on their behalf. Amen.

CONVINCING THE WORLD OF SIN

"I will send [the Counselor] to you.
And when he comes, he will convince the world of its sin."

JOHN 16:7–8

The one object of Christ's coming was to take away sin. The first work of the Spirit in the world is conviction of sin. Without that no real conversion is possible. Pray that the gospel may be preached in such power that men may see that they have rejected and crucified Christ and come to know His saving grace.

Pray most earnestly for a mighty power of conviction of sin wherever the gospel is preached.

Take hold of God's strength when you pray. Read what Isaiah wrote. "These enemies will be spared only if they surrender and beg for peace and protection" (Isaiah 27:5). "Yet no one calls on your name or pleads with you for mercy" (Isaiah 64:7). Paul adds, "Fan into flames the spiritual gift God gave you" (2 Timothy 1:6).

First, take hold of God's strength. God is a Spirit. I cannot take hold of Him except by the Spirit. Take hold of God's strength and hold on until He has done for you what He has promised.

Second, by the Holy Spirit's power in you, fan the flame of intercession in you. Give your whole heart and will to it.

Dear Jesus, in love and concern for the lost, I ask that You stir up a mighty power of conviction of sin wherever the gospel is preached. For Your name's sake, amen.

THE SPIRIT OF BURNING

He will cleanse. . .
by a spirit of judgment that burns like fire.

ISAIAH 4:4

A washing by fire! A cleansing by judgment! Those that have passed through this will be called holy. The power of intercession and blessing for the world depends upon the spiritual state of the Church. Judgment must begin at the house of God; there must be conviction of sin for sanctification. Plead with God to give His Spirit as a spirit of judgment and a spirit of burning—to discover and burn out sin in His people.

Pray in the name of Christ, for He said, "You can ask for anything in my name, and I will do it. . . . Yes, ask anything in my name, and I will do it!" (John 14:13–14).

Ask in the name of your Redeemer God, who sits upon the throne. Ask what He has promised—what He gave His blood for—that sin may be put away from among His people. Ask—the prayer is after His own heart—for the spirit of deep conviction of sin to come to His people. Ask for the spirit of burning. Ask in the faith of His name—the faith of what He will and of what He can do. Then look for the answer. Pray that the Church may be blessed and be a blessing in the world.

O God, in a world that denies the very existence of sin, by the power of Your Spirit give us the mercy of deep conviction of sin so that men may be saved, for Jesus' sake. Amen.

THE CHURCH OF THE FUTURE

Then [each generation] will not be like their ancestors—
stubborn, rebellious and unfaithful,
refusing to give their hearts to God.

PSALM 78:8

P ray for the next generation who are to come after us. Isaiah wrote, "I will pour out my spirit and my blessings on your children" (Isaiah 44:3). Think of the young men and young women and children today and pray for all the special organizations that work with them. Pray that wherever they are Christ may be honored and the Holy Spirit get possession of them.

Pray with your whole heart. "May [the Lord] grant your heart's desire. . ." (Psalm 20:4). "You have given him his heart's desire" (Psalm 21:2). "I pray with all my heart; answer me, LORD!" (Psalm 119:145).

God listens to every request with His whole heart. Each time we pray the whole infinite God is there to hear. He asks that in each prayer the whole person will be there, too, and that we pray with our whole heart. If once we seek God with our whole heart, the whole heart will be in every prayer with which we come to God. Pray with your whole heart for our young people.

Father, shed abroad Your love in the hearts of young people. Remove all unbelief and self-centeredness and grant them a vision of what true faith means—the power of a love which lives for others. In Jesus' name, amen.

SCHOOLS AND COLLEGES

"These words I have given you. . .
will be on your lips and on the lips of your children
and your children's children forever."

ISAIAH 59:21

The future of the Church and the world depends on today's education. The Church may be seeking to evangelize unbelievers but is giving up her own children to secular and materialistic influences. Pray for schools and colleges and for godly teachers. The Church also has a duty to care for its children.

Do not limit God in your prayers. It is a fearful thing to do so. "They tested God's patience and frustrated the Holy One of Israel" (Psalm 78:41). Jesus "did only a few miracles there because of their unbelief" (Matthew 13:58). However, apart from such unbelief, God is not limited. "Is anything too hard for the LORD?" (Genesis 18:14). "O Sovereign LORD! You have made the heavens and earth by your great power. Nothing is too hard for you. . . . 'I am the LORD. . . . Is there anything too hard for me?' " (Jeremiah 32:17, 27).

Beware of limiting God in your prayer, not only by unbelief but by pretending that you know what He can do. Expect unexpected things, greater than all we ask or think. Each time you intercede, be quiet first and worship God. Acknowledge what He can do and expect great things.

Father, in Your unlimited power, we pray for the schools and colleges. Convict teachers of their need for You. Protect our children from godless influences. In Jesus' name, amen.

Sunday Schools

The captives of warriors will be released,
and the plunder of tyrants will be retrieved.
For I will fight those who fight you,
and I will save your children.

Isaiah 49:25

Every part of the work of God's Church is His work. He must do it. Prayer is acknowledging that He will. It is the surrender of ourselves into His hands to let Him work in us and through us. Pray for hundreds of thousands of Sunday school teachers who know God that they may be filled with His Spirit. Pray for your own Sunday school. Pray for the salvation of the children.

Pray boldly. "We have a great High Priest. . .Jesus the Son of God. . . . So let us come boldly to the throne of our gracious God" (Hebrews 4:14, 16).

As we have been thinking about the work of intercession, what is it doing for us? Does it make us aware of our weakness in prayer? Thank God for this. It is the very first lesson we need on the way to praying the "earnest prayer of a righteous person [that] has great power and wonderful results" (James 5:16). Let us persevere taking each item boldly to the throne of grace. As we pray, we shall learn to pray, to believe, and to expect with increasing boldness. Hold fast your confidence; it is at God's command you come as an intercessor. Christ will give you grace to pray as you should.

Lord, hear our prayer for Sunday school teachers. May they have such an experience of Your love that they can proclaim the gospel with power. Let their students know that the life of God is available to them. For Christ's sake. Amen.

KINGS AND RULERS

Pray for all people.
As you make your requests, plead for God's mercy upon them,
and give thanks.

1 TIMOTHY 2:1

O ur text is an example of real faith in the power of prayer! A few weak and despised Christians are to influence the mighty Roman emperors and help secure peace and quietness. Prayer is a power that is honored by God in His rule of the world. Let us pray for our country and its rulers, for all the rulers of the world, for rulers in cities or districts in which we are interested. When God's people unite, they can count upon their prayer affecting the unseen world more than they know.

Prayer is an incense before God. "Then another angel with a gold incense burner came and stood at the altar. And a great quantity of incense was given to him to mix with the prayers of God's people, to be offered on the gold altar before the throne. The smoke of the incense, mixed with the prayers of the saints, ascended up to God from the altar where the angel had poured them out. Then the angel filled the incense burner with fire from the altar and threw it down upon the earth; and thunder crashed, lightning flashed, and there was a terrible earthquake" (Revelation 8:3–5).

The same incense burner brings the prayers of the saints before God and throws fire upon the earth. The prayers that go up to heaven have their share in the history of this earth. Be assured that your prayers enter God's presence.

May those in authority over us, Lord, know the wisdom of Your Spirit
and govern in righteousness. In Jesus' name, amen.

Pray for Peace

[He] causes wars to end throughout the earth.

PSALM 46:9

The military armaments in which the nations find their pride are a terrible sight! The evil passions that may at any moment bring on war are a terrible thought! The suffering and desolation that come from war are a sad prospect!

"I urge you, first of all, to pray. . .for kings and all others who are in authority, so that we can live in peace and quietness, in godliness and dignity. This is good and pleases God our Savior" (1 Timothy 2:1–3). God can, in answer to the prayer of His people, give peace. Let us pray for it and for the rule of righteousness.

When you pray, pray with the understanding. "I will pray in the spirit, and I will pray in words I understand" (1 Corinthians 14:15).

We need to pray in the Spirit if we are to take hold of God in faith and power. We need to pray with understanding if we are really to enter deeply into the needs we bring before Him. Be careful to understand the nature, the extent, the urgency of the request. Comprehend the certainty of God's promise as revealed in His Word. Let the mind affect the heart. Pray with understanding and in the Spirit.

Father, the world seems full of wars and fighting. I long for the peace of Your kingdom in heaven. Please give us peace here on earth. Amen.

THE MISTAKE

"Remain in me, and I will remain in you."

JOHN 15:4

A person thinks, I have my business, family, and community responsibilities. In addition I am to serve God in order to keep from sin. I hope God will help me.

That is not right. When Christ came He bought you with His blood. In those days there was slavery. If someone bought a slave, the slave was required to take orders from his master. The slave lived as if he had no will or interests of his own. His one responsibility was to promote the well-being of his master.

In a similar manner, I have been purchased with the blood of Christ. I am to live every day with one thought, "How can I please my Master?"

We find the Christian life so difficult because we seek for God's blessing while we live life according to our own desires. We make our own plans and choose our own work. Then we ask the Lord to help us not to go too far wrong. Instead, our relationship with Jesus should be that we are entirely at His disposal. We should ask Him daily, "Lord, is there anything in me that is not according to Your will, that is not entirely surrendered to You?"

If we will wait patiently for His guidance there will spring up a relationship between us and Christ so close that we will be amazed. He will take actual possession of us and give us unbroken fellowship.

Dear Lord, total surrender to You is contrary to my natural tendencies. Enable me to entrust my life to You without reservation and to know the close relationship with You that You desire. In Jesus' name, amen.

THE UNREACHED

See, my people will return from far away, from. . .
as far south as Egypt.

ISAIAH 49:12

Will the unreached come to Christ? Does God have such a plan? "Let Egypt come with gifts of precious metals; let Ethiopia bow in submission to God" (Psalm 68:31). " 'I, the LORD, will bring all to pass at the right time' " (Isaiah 60:22).

Pray for those who are yet without the Word: China with her hundreds of millions without Christ; India with its millions; millions each year living in darkness. If Christ gave His life for them, you can give yourself up to intercede for them.

If you have not started to intercede, begin now. God's Spirit will draw you on. Persevere, however hesitant you are. Ask God to give you some country or people group to pray for. Can anything be nobler than to do as Christ did—to give your life for the unreached?

Pray with confident expectation of an answer. "Ask me and I will tell you some remarkable secrets about what is going to happen here" (Jeremiah 33:3). "This is what the Sovereign LORD says: I am ready to hear Israel's prayers. . .and I am ready to grant them their requests" (Ezekiel 36:37). Both texts refer to promises definitely made, but their fulfillment would depend upon prayer.

Father, I pray for God's fulfillment of Your promises to Your Son and the Church. Bring the unreached to Yourself. I ask in Jesus' name, amen.

GOD'S SPIRIT ON ISRAEL

*"Then I will pour out a spirit of grace and prayer
on the family of David and on all the people of Jerusalem.
They will look on me whom they have pierced."*

ZECHARIAH 12:10

D ear friends, the longing of my heart and my prayer to God
is that the Jewish people might be saved" (Romans 10:1).
Paul states his desire for the well-being of Israel. Pray for them.
Their return to the God of their fathers stands connected, in a way
we cannot understand, with wonderful blessing to the Church and
with the coming of our Lord Jesus. Don't think that God has fore-
ordained all this and that we cannot hasten it. In a divine and mysterious way God has connected the fulfillment of His promise
with our prayer. His Spirit's intercession in us is God's forerunner
of blessing. Pray for Israel and the work done among them. Pray,
too: "Amen! Come, Lord Jesus!" (Revelation 22:20).

Pray with the intercession of the Holy Spirit. "We don't
even know what we should pray for, nor how we should pray.
But the Holy Spirit prays for us with groanings that cannot be
expressed in words" (Romans 8:26).

In our ignorance and weakness we can believe in the secret
intercession of the Holy Spirit within us. Habitually yield yourself
to His life and leading. He will help your weakness in prayer. Plead
the promises of God even where you do not see how they are to
be fulfilled. God knows the mind of the Spirit because "the Spirit
pleads for us believers in harmony with God's own will" (Romans
8:27). Pray with the simplicity of a little child; pray with the holy
awe and reverence of one in whom God's Spirit dwells and prays.

*I will ever be in awe, Lord, when I think of the reality of Your spirit
indwelling me. Holy Spirit, thank You for empowering me by praying
in ways I cannot understand. Amen.*

THE SUFFERING

*Share the sorrow of those being mistreated,
as though you feel their pain in your own bodies.*

HEBREWS 13:3

We live in a world of suffering! The persecuted believers in Islamic countries, the famine-stricken millions, those in poverty and wretchedness, refugees from armed conflict—and so much more. In our smaller circles, in thousands of homes and hearts, there is great sorrow! In our own neighborhood, how many need help or comfort? Let us have a heart for the suffering. Jesus sacrificed all and identified Himself with our suffering! Let us in our measure do so, too. It will stir us to pray, to work, to hope, to love more. And in a way and time we do not understand, God will hear our prayers.

Pray always without giving up. "Jesus told his disciples a story to illustrate their need for constant prayer and to show them that they must never give up" (Luke 18:1).

Have you begun to feel that prayer is really the help needed for this sinful world? The very greatness of the task makes us despair! What can our ten minutes of intercession accomplish? It is okay that we feel this: It may be the way in which God is calling and preparing us to give more of our time to prayer. Give yourself wholly to God, pour out your heart to others in love, and look to God in dependence and expectation. To a heart thus led by the Holy Spirit, it is possible to pray always and not give up.

Lord Jesus, help me to see the world as You see it and to pray with compassion and without ceasing. May I not give up. Amen.

The Spirit in Your Own Work

I work very hard at this,
as I depend on Christ's mighty power that works within me.

COLOSSIANS 1:29

You have your own special work; make it a work of intercession. Paul worked hard, depending on God's power working in him. Remember, God not only created us but works in us. You can do your work only in His strength—by Him working in you through the Spirit.

Intercede often for those you work with and for other believers, too. Pray in God's very presence. "Draw close to God, and God will draw close to you" (James 4:8).

The nearness of God gives rest and power in prayer. The nearness of God is given to those who make it their first aim to "Draw close to God." Seek His nearness, and He will give it. "He will draw close to you." Then it becomes easy to pray in faith.

Remember that when first God takes you into the school of intercession, it is almost more for your own sake than that of others. You have to be trained to love and wait and pray and believe. Only persevere. Learn to place yourself in His presence, to wait quietly for the assurance that He draws near. Enter His holy presence, wait there, and bring your concerns before Him.

Father, help me to draw close to You—there can be no more blessed experience. Enable me to experience it. Amen.

THE LOCAL CHURCH

"Beginning in Jerusalem. . ."

LUKE 24:47

Most of us are connected with some church congregation—a community of believers. They are to us the part of Christ's body with which we come into most direct contact. They have a special claim on our intercession. Let it be a settled matter between God and you that you are to intercede on their behalf. Pray for the minister and all leaders and workers. Pray for the believers according to their needs. Pray for conversions. Pray for the power of the Spirit to manifest itself. Join with others in specific prayer. Let intercession be a definite work, carried on as systematically as preaching or Bible studies. And pray, expecting an answer.

Pray continually. Read the Scriptures. "Watchmen. . .will pray to the LORD day and night. . . . Take no rest, all you who pray" (Isaiah 62:6). "His chosen people who plead with him day and night" (Luke 18:7). "Night and day we pray earnestly for you. . ." (1 Thessalonians 3:10). "But a woman who is a true widow, one who is truly alone in this world, has placed her hope in God. Night and day she asks God for help and spends much time in prayer" (1 Timothy 5:5).

When the glory of God, and the love of Christ, and the needs of others are revealed to us, the fire of this unceasing intercession will begin to burn in us for those who are near and those who are far away.

Holy Spirit, please come upon my church with the spirit of revival. Fill our pastor so that we may see Your power work in and through him. In Jesus' name, amen.

The Salvation of Souls

Therefore he is able, once and forever,
to save everyone who comes to God through him.
He lives forever to plead with God on their behalf.

HEBREWS 7:25

Christ's power to save depends on unceasing intercession. "Then we can spend our time in prayer and preaching and teaching the Word. . . . God's message was preached in ever-widening circles. The number of believers greatly increased" (Acts 6:4, 7). After the apostles spent time away in continual prayer, the number of the disciples multiplied greatly.

As we spend time in intercession, we will see more conversions. Christ is exalted as sinners repent. The Church exists with the divine purpose and promise of conversions. Don't be ashamed to confess our sin and weakness and pray to God for more conversions both here and in other countries. Plead for the salvation of sinners.

Pray in deep humility. " 'Yes, Lord. . .but even dogs are permitted to eat crumbs.' . . .'Woman. . .your faith is great. Your request is granted' " (Matthew 15:27–28).

True humility proves its integrity by not seeking for anything but simply trusting His grace. And so it is the strength of a great faith. Don't let your littleness hinder you for a moment.

Lord Jesus, thank You for humbling Yourself and becoming a man.
May I learn from You and come before You in true humility, trusting
You to answer my prayers. Amen.

YOUNG CONVERTS

As soon as [Peter and John] arrived,
they prayed for these new Christians to receive the Holy Spirit.
The Holy Spirit had not yet come upon any of them.

ACTS 8:15–16

M any new converts remain weak, many fall into sin, and
many backslide entirely. As you pray for the Church, its
growth in holiness and devotion to God, pray especially for the
young converts. Many stand alone, surrounded by temptation.
Many have no teaching on the Spirit in them and the power of
God to establish them. They don't know the promise of Scripture: "It is God who gives us, along with you, the ability to stand
firm for Christ. . . . He has identified us as his own by placing
the Holy Spirit in our hearts. . ." (2 Corinthians 1:21–22).
Many are in other countries, surrounded by Satan's power. Pray
for the power of the Spirit in the Church and especially that
every young convert may know the fullness of the Spirit.

Pray without ceasing. " 'As for me, I will certainly not sin
against the LORD by ending my prayers for you' " (1 Samuel
12:23).

It is sin against the Lord to stop praying for others. Once
we begin to see how indispensable intercession is—just as much
a duty as loving God—we will feel that to stop intercession is
sin. Ask for grace to fill the role of intercessor with joy and give
our life to bring down the blessings of heaven.

Lord God, be with those young converts who have little knowledge of
Your Word. Fill them with the Holy Spirit. May they learn to delight
in the Scriptures. In Jesus' name, amen.

REALIZE OUR CALLING

*"I will bless you. . .and make you a blessing to others. . . .
All the families of the earth will be blessed through you."*

GENESIS 12:2–3

Abraham was only blessed that he might be a blessing to all the earth. Israel prays for blessing that God may be known among all nations. Every believer, just as much as Abraham, is blessed so that he may carry God's blessing to the world. "May God be merciful and bless us. May his face shine with favor upon us. May your ways be known throughout the earth, your saving power among people everywhere" (Psalm 67:1–2).

Plead with God that His people may know that every believer is only to live for the interests of God and His kingdom. If this truth were preached and believed and practiced, it would bring dramatic changes in our mission work. We would have a host of willing intercessors.

Pray as one who has accepted for himself what he asks for others. "The Holy Spirit fell on them, just as he fell on us at the beginning. . . . God gave these Gentiles the same gift he gave us" (Acts 11:15, 17).

As you pray for the Holy Spirit to take entire possession of God's people for God's service, yield yourself to God and claim the gift anew in faith. As the blessing comes to others, you, too, will be helped.

Lord, as You have blessed me, make me a blessing. Use me, use Your Church, for the blessing of the earth. Amen.

KNOW THE HOLY SPIRIT

Don't you know that your body is
the temple of the Holy Spirit. . . ?

1 CORINTHIANS 6:19

The Holy Spirit is the power of God for the salvation of men. He only works as He dwells in the Church. He is given to enable believers to live as God wants them to live—in the full experience and witness of Him who saves completely.

Ask God for every one of His people to know the Holy Spirit! They cannot expect to live as their Father desires without having Him in His fullness, without being filled with Him! Pray that all God's people may learn to say: "I believe in the Holy Spirit."

Pray earnestly. "Epaphras, from your city. . .sends you his greetings. He always prays earnestly for you, asking God to make you strong and perfect, fully confident of the whole will of God" (Colossians 4:12).

To a healthy man work is a delight; he works earnestly in what interests him. The believer who is in good spiritual health, whose heart is filled with God's Spirit, prays earnestly. For what?—that believers may stand perfect and complete in all the will of God, that they may know what God wills for them, and walk by the Holy Spirit.

Dear God, may every one of us, Your people, know the Holy Spirit.
May we know that He is given to us and that in His power we can
live a life of power and spiritual effectiveness. Amen.

THE SPIRIT OF INTERCESSION

*"I chose you. I appointed you to go and produce fruit. . .
so that the Father will give you whatever you ask for,
using my name."*

JOHN 15:16

Often our intercession lacks power because we have not prayed in the name of Jesus. He promised His disciples that when the Holy Spirit came upon them, they could ask for anything in His name. Let us intercede today for all God's children that Christ may teach them that the Holy Spirit is in them. May He teach us what it is to live in His fullness and to yield ourselves to His work of intercession within us. The Church and the world need nothing as much as a mighty Spirit of intercession to bring down the power of God on earth. Pray for the Spirit of intercession to bring a great prayer revival.

Pray, joined to Christ. "If you stay joined to me and my words remain in you, you may ask any request you like, and it will be granted" (John 15:7).

Our acceptance with God—our access to Him—is all in Christ. As we consciously abide in Him we have the liberty to ask what we will in the power of the new nature, and it will be done.

Almighty God, as I abide in You, teach me what it means. May I not be limited by self but free to be all You have for me. In Jesus' name, amen.

THE WORD OF GOD

It was not only with words but also with power,
for the Holy Spirit gave you full assurance that
what we said was true.

1 THESSALONIANS 1:5

Many Bibles are being circulated. Many sermons on the Bible are being preached. Many Bibles are being read. The blessing comes not just in words only. The blessing and power comes in the Holy Spirit, when it is preached with the Holy Spirit. "This Good News has been announced by those who preached to you in the power of the Holy Spirit sent from heaven" (1 Peter 1:12).

Pray for the power of the Spirit through the Word in all the world wherever it is being read or heard. Let every mention of the Word of God call us to intercession.

Be alert and pray. "Devote yourselves to prayer with an alert mind and a thankful heart. Don't forget to pray for us, too, that God will give us many opportunities to preach. . ." (Colossians 4:2–3).

Do you see how everything depends upon God and prayer? As long as He lives and loves and hears and works, as long as there are hearts closed to the Word, as long as there is work to be done in carrying the Word—pray at all times.

Lord God, unless Your Word is illuminated with the light of Your Spirit, it doesn't change the direction of lives. But with Your Spirit, it is sharp and powerful. Send Your Spirit to men and women who read Your Word so that they may have the privilege of rightly responding to it and of knowing You. In Jesus' name, amen.

CHRIST IN HIS PEOPLE

"Yes, I am the vine; you are the branches. . . .
But if you stay joined to me and my words remain in you,
you may ask any request you like,
and it will be granted!"

JOHN 15:5, 7

A s branches we are to be so like the vine, so entirely identified with it, that everyone may see that we have the same nature and life and spirit. When we pray for the Spirit, let us not only think of a Spirit of power, but the very attitude of Christ Jesus. Ask and expect nothing less for yourself and all God's children.

What must we be or do that will enable us to pray as we should and to receive what we ask? The answer is this: It is the branch life that gives power for prayer. We are branches of Christ, the living vine. We must simply live like branches and abide in Christ; then we shall ask what we will and it shall be done for us.

Struggle in prayer. "Join me in my struggle by praying to God for me" (Romans 15:30). "I want you to know how much I have agonized for you. . ." (Colossians 2:1).

All the powers of evil seek to hinder us in prayer. Prayer is a conflict with opposing forces. It needs our whole heart and all our strength. May God give us grace to struggle in prayer until we have victory.

As a branch of the vine I come to You, Lord. Thank You that You are in me, and that I am in You. Enable me to live as a branch that depends totally on the vine. In Jesus' name, amen.

THE LOST STANDARD

"Do not leave Jerusalem until the Father
sends you what he promised. . . .
In just a few days you will be baptized with the Holy Spirit."

ACTS 1:4–5

After Jesus had given the command to go into all the world and preach the gospel to every creature, He added His very last command: "Do not leave Jerusalem until the Father sends you what he promised. . . . In just a few days you will be baptized with the Holy Spirit."

Christians agree that the command to preach the gospel was not only for the disciples but is for us, too. But not everyone considers that this last command is also for us. The Church appears to have lost possession of its secret—the awareness that it is only by living in the power of the Holy Spirit that the gospel can be preached in power. Because of this there is a lot of preaching and working with very few spiritual results. There is little prayer that brings down God's power.

For the next several days we will study the secret of Pentecost as it is found in the words and deeds of our Master and His disciples. They continued with one accord in prayer until the promise was fulfilled. Then they became full of the Holy Spirit and proved what the power of God could do.

Holy Spirit, reveal to me what eye has not seen, nor ear heard, nor has my heart conceived—the things which God loves to do for those that wait upon Him. Help me find the lost secret—that in answer to fervent prayer the power of the Holy Spirit will be given. I ask in Jesus' name, amen.

THE KINGDOM OF GOD

*During the forty days after his crucifixion,
he appeared to the apostles from time to time. . . .
On these occasions he talked to them about the kingdom of God.*

ACTS 1:3

W hen Christ began to preach, He repeated the message of
John that the kingdom of heaven was near. Later He said:
"Some of you standing here right now will not die before you see
the kingdom of God arrive in great power!" (Mark 9:1). That
could not happen until the King had taken His throne. Then His
disciples were ready to receive the gift of the Holy Spirit, bringing down the kingdom of God in its heavenly power.

Our text tells us that all the teaching of Jesus after the resurrection dealt with the kingdom of God. Luke sums up all the
teaching of Paul at Rome: He proclaimed the kingdom of God
(Acts 28:31).

Christ, seated upon the throne, was now King and Lord of
all. He had entrusted to His disciples the announcement of the
kingdom. The prayer He had taught them, "Our Father in
heaven. . .may your Kingdom come soon" (Matthew 6:9–10),
now had a new meaning for them: The kingdom of God as seen
in heaven came down in the power of the Spirit. There was now
on earth good news of the kingdom of God ruling and dwelling
with men, even as in heaven.

*Lord Jesus, please give me wisdom to understand You and Your king-
dom. Give to me the power of the Holy Spirit so that I can do the work
You have entrusted to me. Help me to be persistent in prayer as I seek
to proclaim the good news of Your kingdom. Amen.*

CHRIST AS KING

*"I assure you that some of you standing here
right now will not die before you see
the Kingdom of God arrive in great power!"*

MARK 9:1

Christ said that it would be in the lifetime of some who heard Him that the kingdom would come in power. That meant that when He, as King, had ascended the throne of the Father, the kingdom would be revealed in the hearts of His disciples. In the kingdom of heaven God's will is always being done. Christ's disciples would do His will even as it was done in heaven.

We can see in the King the mark of what a kingdom is. Christ was now on the throne of the Father. On earth its power is seen in the lives of those it rules. Only in them the united Body can be seen. Jesus Himself taught how close the relationship would be. "On that day you will realize that I am in my Father, and you are in Me, and I am in you."

This is our first lesson. We must know that Christ rules in our hearts as King. We must know that in His power we are able to accomplish all that He wants us to do. Our whole life is to be devoted to our King and the service of His kingdom. This comes only through consistent daily prayer.

Lord Jesus Christ, I hunger for daily fellowship with You in prayer. May my prayer life be a continuous and unbroken exercise. I rejoice in You, my King, and know that in You I can be more than conqueror. In Your name, amen.